BASIC JAPANESE CONVERSATION DICTIONARY

by the same author

EASY JAPANESE

ESSENTIAL JAPANESE

KOREAN IN A HURRY

BASIC JAPANESE CONVERSATION DICTIONARY

(***English-Japanese***
Japanese-English)

Revised and Enlarged

by

SAMUEL E. MARTIN

Professor of Far Eastern Linguistics

Yale University

CHARLES E. TUTTLE CO.
Rutland, Vermont
Tokyo, Japan

Representatives
For Continental Europe:
BOXERBOOKS, INC., *Zurich*
For the British Isles:
PRENTICE-HALL INTERNATIONAL, INC., *London*
For Australasia:
BOOK WISE (AUSTRALIA) PTY. LTD.
104–108 Sussex Street, Sydney 2000

Published by the Charles E. Tuttle Company, Inc.
of Rutland, Vermont & Tokyo, Japan
with editorial offices at
Suido 1-chome, 2-6, Bunkyo-ku, Tokyo

Library of Congress Catalog Card No. 57-8797

International Standard Book No. 0-8048-0057-X

First printing, 1957
Second printing, 1958
Second edition (revised
and enlarged), 1959
Sixty-third printing, 1985

Printed in Japan

CONTENTS

Introduction vii

Part I
English-Japanese 3

Part II
Japanese-English 129

Part III
Writing Charts. 263

Part IV
Money Conversion Tables 269

CONTENTS

Introduction vii

Part I

English-Japanese 3

Part II

Japanese-English 129

Part III

Writing Charts 263

Part IV

Money Conversion Tables 269

INTRODUCTION

This dictionary has a purely practical aim. That is to put you into immediate communication with Japanese who speak little or no English. You will find 3000 useful English words with their most common Japanese equivalents. Only the most frequent meanings of the English words have been included; naturally, each English word has many other meanings. But the chances are, the meaning you want is the one given here. When the Japanese equivalent is a verb, it is given in the polite present form: **-mas'** "does" or "will do." From this form the polite past and the polite suggestion forms are easily made: **-mash'ta** "did" or "has done"; **-mashō** "let's do" or "I think I'll do." In parentheses are given the PLAIN present form (**-u** or **-ru**), and the gerund (**-te** or **-de** "doing" or "does and"). From the gerund, you can make the plain past tense by changing **-te** or **-de** to **-ta** or **-da.** Some English adjectives correspond to Japanese nouns, and these fall into two categories: ordinary nouns, which link to a following noun with the word **no**; and copular nouns, which link to a following noun with the word **na.** Copular nouns are shown in this dictionary by adding **na** in parentheses: **genki (na).** Ordinary nouns are sometimes given with **no** in parentheses to show they correspond to English adjectives but are not copular nouns.

Some of the words are preceded by three dots. This means that you put in front of them the words that would come after the corresponding English. For example English "in" would be followed by, let us say, "America." But the corresponding Japanese word **ni** would be preceded by **Amerika:** "in America" would be **"Amerika ni."**

If you have trouble pronouncing the Japanese words, just look up the English word you want to express, and point to the Japanese writing. Your Japanese friend will then be able to figure out what you are trying to say. If you can't find the word you want, try to think of some other common English word that means the same thing, and look that up. If it isn't in the dictionary either, then try using the English word right in the middle of your Japanese.

The Japanese is presented in a slightly modified form of the Hepburn romanization. Most of the consonants are pronounced about as in English, the vowels as in Italian: **a** as in f*a*ther, **e** as in m*e*t or y*e*s, **i** as in mar*i*ne or macaron*i*, **o** as in sol*o* or

P*ogo*, **u** as in r*u*le or L*u*l*u*. These vowels are shorter than our English vowels; the long varieties (marked **ā, ō, ū, ii,** and either **ei** or **ē**) are a little longer and tenser than the English sounds like them. In everyday speech, many final long vowels are shortened. The apostrophe (as in **s'koshi arimas'**) represents a short **u** (after **s, k,** etc.) or **i** (after **sh, ch**) which is suppressed in ordinary speech. You will find **s'** alphabetized as if it were **su, sh'** as if it were **shi** You may hear other vowels suppressed occasionally. The tongue is pushed farther forward (against the teeth) for Japanese **t, d,** and **n** than for the English sounds. The Japanese **r** may sound like a combination of **r, l,** and **d** to you. Your English **d** (if you say it very quickly) is probably the closest. But don't mix it up with a Japanese **d!** The Japanese **g** never has the "soft" *j*-sound as in *g*em or *g*in; it is either "hard" as in *g*et or *g*ift or it has the "ng" sound in sin*g*er. If you have trouble with the "ng" version, forget it and use the "hard" **g** everywhere. The **n** which comes at the end of a word sounds a little bit like a weak "ng" instead of a full-fledged **n**; try to imitate this if you hear the difference.

In the Japanese-English part, the Japanese verbs are presented both in the polite present (**-mas'**) and the plain present (**-u** or **-ru**). When the two forms would come close together in alphabetical order, they are given on one line; in other cases, you will find two entries.

The beginner will find he can take the Japanese equivalents of English words (skipping the little, unimportant English words) and string them together much as he does in English. The Japanese will understand him most of the time, even though the effect is choppy. If you want to find out more about how to put the words together in sentences, you will find it useful to get the author's other two works, EASY JAPANESE and ESSENTIAL JAPANESE. This dictionary should be a useful supplement for students using these two textbooks.

In order to make this book a handy size it was necessary to restrict the number of words and the amount of explanatory materials included. The author would be happy to hear of any omissions which particularly trouble you as you use the book.

PART I

English-Japanese

NOTE: The Japanese equivalents are given both in Romanization and in native writing. If you wish, you can find the English word you want to communicate and point to the Japanese equivalent, letting your Japanese friends pronounce it themselves. In the Romanized part, each verb is given in the polite present (**-mas'**) with the plain present (**-u**) and the gerund (**-te**) following in parentheses. In the native writing only the plain present is given. This is the form in which the verbs appear in Japanese dictionaries.

A

a, an *see* one (*but usually omitted in Japanese*)
abacus **soroban** そろばん
abandon **s'temas'** (*s'teru, s'tete*) 捨てる
abbreviate **ryaku-shimas'** (*-su, -sh'te*) 略す
abbreviation **ryakugo** 略語
abhor *see* hate
ability **sai** 才
able *see* can
abolish **haishi shimas'** (*suru, sh'te*) 廃止する
abortion **datai** 堕胎
about (a certain amount) **yaku...** 約 *or* **...gurai** ぐらい; *see also* almost, around
about (a certain time) **...goro (ni)** ごろ(に)
about (*concerning*) **...ni tsuite (no)** について(の)
(talk) about **...(no) koto o iimas'** (*yū, itte or yutte*) の事を言う
above **...(no) ue (ni)** (の) 上 (に)
abroad **gaikoku (de)** 外国 (で)
abrupt **totsuzen** 突然
absent **rusu (des')** 留守 (です)
absent-minded **bon-yari shimas'** (*suru, sh'te*) ぼんやりする
absolutely **honto ni** ほんとに
absurd **baka-rashii** ばからしい
abuse *see* scold
A.C. current **kōryū** 交流

accent **ak'sento** アクセント; *see also* pronunciation, dialect
accept **moraimas'** (*morau, moratte*) 貰う
accessible (*easy to get to*) **iki-yasui** 行きやすい
accident **jiko** 事故 *or* **dekigoto** 出來事
accidentally **gūzen ni** 偶然に
accomodations (*place to stay*) **tomaru tokoro** 泊まる所
accompany (**...to**) **issho ni ikimas'** (*iku, itte*) (と)一緒に行く; **o-tomo shimas'** (*suru, sh'te*) お供する
accomplish **(sh'te) shimaimas'** (*shimau, shimatte*) (して)しまう
according to **. . . ni yoru to** によると
account (*bill*) **kanjō** 勘定
(on) account of *see* because
accountant **kaikei** 会計
accumulate (*it accumulates*) **atsumarimas'** (*atsumaru, atsumatte*) 集まる; (*accumulates it*) **atsumemas'** (*atsumeru, atsumete*) 集める
accurate **seikaku (na)** 精確(な)
accuse **hinan shimas'** (*suru, sh'te*) 非難する
accustom oneself to **. . . ni naremas'** (*nareru, narete*) に慣れる
ache **itamimas'** (*itamu, itande*) 痛む
acid **san (no)** 酸(の)
acknowledge **mitomemas'** (*mitomeru, mitomete*) 認める
acquaintance **shiriai** 知り合い
acquainted with **. . . o shitte imas'** (*iru, ite*) を知っている
acquire *see* get

across **. . . (no) mukō ni** (の) 向うに
act *see* do
action, activity **katsudō** 活動
activity (*agency*) **kikan** 機関
actor **haiyū** 俳優
actress **joyū** 女優
actually **jitsu wa** 実は *or* **jitsu ni** 実に
acute (*sharp*) **surudoi** 鋭い; (*severe*) **hageshii** 烈しい; (*sudden*) **kyūsei (no)** 急性 (の)
ad *see* advertisement
add **kuwaemas'** (*kuwaeru, kuwaete*) 加える
additional *see* more
address **tokoro** 所; (*house number*) **banchi** 番地; (*written*) **tokoro-gaki** 所書き *or* **ate-na** 宛名
adequate *see* enough
adhesive tape **noritsuki-tēpu** のり付きテープ
adjacent *see* next
adjective **keiyōshi** 形容詞
adjoining **tonari (no)** 隣 (の)
adjust **totonoemas'** (*totonoeru, totonoete*) 整える
administration (*of government*) **gyōsei** 行政
admirable **migoto (na)** 見事 (な)
admiral **taishō** 大将; (vice) **chūjō** 中将; (rear) **shōshō** 少将
admire **kanshin shimas'** (*suru, sh'te*) 感心する
admit (*lets in*) **iremas'** (*ireru, irete*) 入れる; (*acknowledges*) **mitomemas'** (*mitomeru, mitomete*) 認める; (*confesses*) **uchi-akemas'** (*-akeru, -akete*) 打ち明ける

adolescence **shishunki** 思春期
adolescent **seinen** 青年
adopt *(a boy)* **yōshi ni shimas'** *(suru, sh'te)* 養子にする; *(a girl)* **yōjo ni shimas'** *(suru, sh'te)* 養女にする
adopted (son) **yōshi** 養子; (daughter) **yōjo** 養女
adore *see* love
adult **otona** 大人
advance **susumimas'** *(susumu, susunde)* 進む
(in) advance **sono mae ni** その前に
advantage **toku** 得; (take ...of) **riyō shimas'** *(suru, sh'te)* 利用する
adventure **bōken** 冒険
adverb **f'kushi** 副詞
advertisement **kōkoku** 広告
advice **sōdan** 相談 *or* **chūkoku** 忠告
adviser *(consultant)* **komon** 顧問
aerial *see* antenna
affair **koto** 事 *or* **jiken** 事件
affect *see* influence
affected **kidotta** 気取った
affection **aijō** 愛情
affliction **kurushimi** 苦しみ
afford **(jūbun na) kane ga arimas'** *(aru, atte)* (十分な) 金がある
afraid (of . . .) **(. . . ga) kowai** こわい
Africa **Afurika** アフリカ
after **(. . . no) ato de** 後で
afternoon **hiru kara** 昼から *or* **gogo** 午後

after-shave (lotion) **as'torinzen** アストリンゼン
again **mō ichi-do** もう一度 *or* **mō ik-kai** もう一回
against (*in contrast to*) **. . . ni taish'te** に対して; (*opposing*) **. . . ni hantai sh'te** に反対して; (*running into*) **. . . ni butsukatte** にぶつかって
age **toshi** 年
agency (*middleman*) **dairi** 代理; (*organization*) **kikan** 機関
agent **dairi** 代理; (*ticket agent*) **kippu-uri** 切符売り
aggravating **haradatashii** 腹立たしい
aggression **shinryaku** 侵略
ago **. . . mae ni** 前に
agony **kurushimi** 苦しみ
agree **sansei shimas'** (*suru, sh'te*) 賛成する
agriculture **nōgyō** 農業
ahead **saki (ni)** 先(に)
aid *see* help
ail *see* sick
aim at **neraimas'** (*nerau, neratte*) 狙う
air **kūki** 空気
air base **kūgun-kichi** 空軍基地
air conditioning **reibō** 冷房
airfield *see* airport
air force **kū-gun** 空軍
air mail **kōkū-bin** 航空便
airman **kōkū-hei** 航空兵
airplane **hikōki** 飛行機
airport **hikōjō** 飛行場

airsick(ness) **hikō-yoi** 飛行酔い

aisle **tsūro** 通路

à la carte **ippin-ryōri** 一品料理

alarm clock **mezamashi-dokei** 目ざまし時計

album (*photograph*) **shashin-chō** 写真帳; (*stamp*) **kitte-chō** 切手帳

alcohol **arukōru** アルコール

alike **onaji** 同じ

alive **ikite imas'** (*iru, ite*) 生きている

all **minna** 皆 *or* **zembu** 全部

alley **yokochō** 横町

Allies **Rengō-koku** 連合国

allow **yurushimas'** (*yurusu, yurush'te*) 許す

allowance (*bonus*) **teate** 手当て

almost **hotondo** ほとんど

alone **hitori** (**de**) 一人(で)

along . . . **. . . no doko ka** (**de**) のどこか(で)

alongside **. . . no soba** のそば

aloud **koe o dash'te** 声を出して

alphabet (*English*) **ē-bii-shii** エービーシー; (*Japanese*) **kana** かな

already **mō** もう

also **. . . mo** も *or* **sono ue** その上

altar **saidan** 祭壇 *or* **seitaku** 聖卓

alter **naoshimas'** (*naosu, naosh'te*) 直す

alternately **kawaru-gawaru** かわるがわる

alternating current *see* AC

although **. . . no ni** のに

altogether **minna de** 皆で

aluminum **arumi(nyūmu)** アルミ(ニューム)

alumnus (of . . .) **(. . . no) shusshin** (の) 出身
always **itsu mo** いつも
am *see* is
. . . a.m. **gozen . . .** 午前
amateur **amachua** アマチュア
ambassador **taishi** 大使
amber **kohaku** こはく
ambition (*hope*) **netsubō** 熱望; (*energetic spirit*) **haki** 覇気
ambulance **kyūkyūsha** 救急車
America **Amerika** アメリカ *or* **Beikoku** 米国
American (person) **Amerika-jin** アメリカ人 *or* **Beikoku-jin** 米国人
ammunition **dan-yaku** 弾薬
among **. . . no naka** (*or* **uchi** *or* **aida**) の中「(内, 間)
amount to (how much) **(ikura) ni narimas'** (*naru, natte*) (いくら)になる
ample *see* enough
amusement **asobi** 遊び
amusing **omoshiroi** おもしろい
an *see* a
analysis **bunseki** 分析
ancestor **senzo** 先祖
anchor **ikari** 錨
ancient **mukashi no** 昔の *or* **kodai no** 古代の
and . . . (*if you are including each item*) **. . . to** と; (*if you are choosing typical items*) **. . . ya** や
(does) and **shi** *or* VERB GERUND (**-te** form)

(is) and **shi** *or* ADJECTIVE GERUND (**-k'te** form)
angel **tenshi** 天使
angle **kakudo** 角度; (*scheme*) **kufū** 工夫
(gets) angry **okorimas'** (*okoru, okotte*) 怒る
animal **dōbutsu** 動物
ankle **ashi-kubi** 足首
anklets **sokkusu** ソックス
annex **bekkan** 別館
anniversary **kinembi** 記念日
announce (*inform*) **shirasemas'** (*shiraseru, shirasete*) 知らせる
announcer **anaunsā** アナウンサー
annoying **urusai** うるさい
another **mō hitotsu** もうひとつ
answer **kotaemas'** (*kotaeru, kotaete*) 答える
ant **ari** あり
antenna **antena** アンテナ
anthropology **jinrui-gaku** 人類学
anti-American **haibei (no)** 排米(の)
antibiotic(s) **taikinsei-yakuzai** 対菌性薬剤
anticipate **machimas'** (*matsu, matte*) 待つ
anti-Communist **hankyō (no)** 反共(の)
antidote **dokkeshi** 毒消し
antifreeze **kōtōketsu-zai** 抗凍結剤
anti-Japanese **hannichi (no)** 反日(の)
antique **jidai-mono** 時代物
antiseptic **bōfu-zai** 防腐剤
anxious *see* worried
any *usually omitted in Japanese*

anybody **hito** 人
anybody (at all) **dare de mo** 誰でも
anyhow (*nevertheless*) **to-ni-kaku** とにかく
anyhow (at all) **dō de mo** どうでも
anyone *see* anybody
anyplace *see* anywhere
any time **itsu de mo** いつでも 「*ten omitted*)
anything (*something*) **nani ka** 何か (*but of-*
anything (at all) **nan de mo** 何でも
anyway *see* anyhow
anywhere (*somewhere*) **doko ka** どこか
anywhere (at all) **doko de mo** どこでも
apartment **apāto** アパート
apiece **. . . zutsu** ずつ
apologize **wabimas'** (*wabiru, wabite*) 詫びる
apparatus **sōchi** 装置
appear **miemas'** (*mieru, miete*) 見える
appetite **shokuyoku** 食欲
apple **ringo** りんご
application (*for job, etc.*) **mōshi-komi** 申込み
appointment *see* date
appreciate **arigataku omoimas'** (*omou, omot-*
te) ありがたく思う 「*zuite*) 近づく
approach **chikazukimas'** (*chikazuku, chika-*
approve **sansei shimas'** (*suru, sh'te*) 賛成する
approximately **daitai** 大体
April **Shi-gatsu** 四月
architecture **kenchiku** 建築
are *see* is

argument **kenka** けんか
arm **te** 手 *or* (*strictly*) **ude** 腕
army **rikugun** 陸軍 ⌈about
around (**. . . no**) **mawari ni** まわりに; *see also*
arrangements **jumbi** 準備
arrive (at) (**ni**) **ts'kimas'** (*ts'ku, tsuite*)(に)着く
art **bijutsu** 美術 *or* **geijutsu** 芸術
article (*thing*) **mono** 物; (*write-up*) **kiji** 記事
as (*like*) (**. . . no**) **yō** (**ni**) (の)様(に)
ashamed **hazukashii** はずかしい
ashes **hai** 灰
ash tray **hai-zara** 灰皿
ask (a person a question) (**. . . ni**) **kikimas'** (*kiku, kiite*) (に)聞く
ask (a favor of a person) (**. . . ni . . . o**) **tanomimas'** (*tanomu, tanonde*) たのむ *or* **negaimas'** (*negau, negatte*) 願う
association **kyōkai** 協会 ⌈*at*) **. . . de** で
at (*being located at*) **. . . ni** に; (*happening*
athlete **senshu** 選手
Atlantic Ocean **Taiseiyō** 大西洋
atmosphere (of a place) **fun-iki** ふんいき
atom **genshi** 原子
atombomb **genshi-bakudan** 原子爆弾
attach **ts'kemas'** (*ts'keru, ts'kete*) 付ける
attack **kōgeki shimas'** (*suru, sh'te*) 攻撃する
attention **chūi** 注意
auditorium **kōdō** 講堂
Australia **Ōs'torariya** オーストラリヤ

Australian (*person*) **Ōs'torariya-jin** オーストラリヤ人
average **heikin** 平均
avoid **sakemas'** (*sakeru, sakete*) 避ける
awake **mezamemas'** (*mezameru, mezamete*) 目ざめる
(go) away **ikimas'** (*iku, itte*) 行く
(take) away **torimas'** (*toru, totte*) 取る
awful **osoroshii** 恐ろしい

B

baby **aka-chan** 赤ちゃん *or* **akambo** 赤んぼ
bachelor **dokushin** 独身 *or* **hitori-mono** 独身者
back (*behind*) **ushiro** うしろ
back (*of body*) **senaka** 背中
bad **warui** 悪い *or* **dame** だめ
bag **fukuro** 袋
baggage **te-nimotsu** 手荷物
bake **yakimas'** (*yaku, yaite*) 焼く
bakery, bakeshop **pan-ya** パン屋
ball **tama** たま *or* **mari** まり
bamboo **take** 竹
bamboo shoots **takenoko** 筍
bandage **hōtai** 繃帯
bank **ginkō** 銀行
bar **saka-ba** 酒場 *or* **bā** バー
barber(shop) **tokoya** 床屋
base (*military*) **kichi** 基地
baseball **yakyū** 野球
basket **kago** 籠 *or* **zaru** ざる

bath, (takes a . . .) **furo** (**ni hairimas'**; ***hairu, haitte***) 風呂 (に入る)
bathing suit **mizugi** 水着
bathroom (*for bathing*) **furo-ba** 風呂場; (*toilet*) **benjo** 便所
battery **denchi** 電池
be *see* is
beach **hama** 浜
bean **mame** 豆
bear (*animal*) **kuma** 熊
beard **hige** ひげ
beat *see* hit; *see* win
beautiful **utsukushii** 美しい
beauty parlor **biyōin** 美容院
because . . . **. . . kara** から *or* **. . . tame** ため
become **. . . ni narimas'** (*naru, natte*) になる
bed **toko** 床; (*American*) **shindai** 寝台
bedroom **ne-ma** 寝間 *or* **shinshitsu** 寝室
bee **mitsu-bachi** 密ばち
beef **gyūniku** 牛肉
beefsteak **bif'teki** ビフテキ
beer **biiru** ビール
before (**. . . no**) **mae** (**ni**) (の)前(に)
beggar **kojiki** 乞食
begin (*it begins*) **hajimarimas'** (*hajimaru, hajimatte*) 始まる; (*begins it*) **hajimemas'** (*hajimeru, hajimete*) 始める
behind (**. . . no**) **ushiro** (**ni**) (の)うしろ(に)
believe **shinjimas'** (*shinjiru, shinjite*) 信じ

る; *see also* think 「(*doorbell*) **beru** ベル
bell (*large*) **kane** かね; (*small*) **rin** りん;
belong (to) (**...ni**) **zoku-shimas'** (*-suru, -sh'te*) (に)属する
below (**...no**) **sh'ta** (**ni**) (の) 下 (に)
belt **bando** バンド *or* **obi** 帯
bend (*it bends*) **magarimas'** (*magaru, magatte*) 曲がる; (*bends it*) **magemas'** (*ma-*
beneath *see* below ⌊*geru, magete*) 曲げる
beside (**...no**) **tonari** (**ni**) (の) となり (に) *or* (**...no**) **waki** (**ni**) (の) 側 (に)
besides **sono ue ni** その上に
best **ichiban ii** 一番いい
bet **kakemas'** (*kakeru, kakete*) かける *or* **kake o shimas'** (*suru, sh'te*) かけをする
better **motto ii** もっといい *or* **...yori ii**
between (**...no**) **aida** (の) 間 ⌊よりいい
beyond (**...no**) **mukō** (の) 向う
Bible **Seisho** 聖書
bicycle **jitensha** 自転車
big **ōkii** 大きい
bill **kanjō** 勘定
billiards **tama-ts'ki** 玉突
bird **ko-tori** 小鳥 *or* **tori** 鳥
birthday **tanjōbi** 誕生日
bit (*a little*) **s'koshi** 少し
bite **kamimas'** (*kamu, kande*) 咬む *or* **kami-ts'kimas'** (*-ts'ku, -tsuite*) かみつく
bitter **nigai** にがい

black **kuroi** 黒い
blanket **mōfu** 毛布
blemish **kizu** きず
blind **mekura** めくら
blindfold **mekakushi** 目隠し
blink **ma-tataki** (*or* **ma-bataki**) **shimas'** (*suru, sh'te*) またたき(まばたき)する
blister **mizu-bukure** 水ぶくれ
blizzard **fubuki** 吹雪
block *The closest Japanese equivalent is* **chōme,** *a square which includes several blocks. For distances,* use **-chō:** It is three blocks from here. **Koko kara san-chō des'.**
blond **kimpatsu** 金髪
blood **chi** 血
bloom **sakimas'** (*saku, saite*) 咲く
bloomers **mompe** モンペ
blot, bloch **shimi** しみ
blotter **suitori-gami** 吸取紙
blouse (*of uniform*) **jaketsu** ジャケツ; (*women's, children's*) **burausu** ブラウス; (*coat*) **uwagi** 上着
blow **f'kimas'** (*f'ku, fuite*) 吹く
blowfish **fugu** ふぐ
blue **aoi** 青い
blueprint **ao-jashin** 青写真
blunt (*dull-edged*) **kirenai** 切れない; *dull-pointed*) **nibui** 鈍い; (*rude*) **busahō** (**na**) 無作法(な)

blush **akaku narimas'** (*naru, natte*) 赤くなる
board **ita** 板
boast **jiman shimas'** (*suru, sh'te*) 自慢する
boat **fune** 船 *or* (*small one*) **kobune** 小舟
bobby soxer **jogak'sei** 女学生
bock beer **kuro-biiru** 黒ビール
body **karada** 体
(gets) bogged (down) **iki-zumarimas'** (*-zumaru, -zumatte*) 行き詰る
boil (on skin) **haremono** はれもの
boiled water (*cooled for drinking*) **yu-zamashi** 湯ざまし
boiler (*for heating water*) **yu-wakashi** 湯わかし; (*pot*) **kama** かま
boils (water) **o-yu o wakashimas'** (*wakasu, wakash'te*) お湯を沸かす
(water) boils **o-yu ga wakimas'** (*waku, waite*) お湯が沸く
boisterous **yakamashii** やかましい *or* **sawagashii** さわがしい
bold **daitan** (na) 大膽(な) *or* **-tan** 反
bolt (*of door*) **kannuki** 閂; (*of cloth*) **-maki** 巻
bomb **bakudan** 爆弾
bomber **bakugeki-ki** 爆撃機
bombing **bakugeki** 爆撃
bond (*debenture*) **saiken**債券
bone **hone** 骨
bonfire **takibi** 焚火
bonito **katsuo** かつお
bonus **shōyo(-kin)** 賞与(金)

book **hon** 本
bookcase **hombako** 本箱
bookends **hon-tate** 本立て
bookie **kakeya (san)** 賭け屋(さん)
bookkeeping **boki** 簿記
bookmark **shiori** しおり
bookshelf **hon-dana** 本棚
bookshop **hon-ya** 本屋
boom (*prosperity*) **keiki** 景気; (*fad*) **būmu** ブーム; (*sound*) **don** どん
booster (*of current*) **shōatsu-ki** 昇圧機
booth (*selling things*) **baiten** 売店; (*telephone*) **denwa-shitsu** 電話室
boots **naga-gutsu** 長靴
border (*edging*) **heri** へり; (*of district, etc.*) **kyōkai** 境界; (*of country*) **kokkyō** 国境
boring (*dull*) **taikutsu (na)** 退屈(な) 「生れる
(is) born **umaremas'** (*umareru, umarete*)
borrow **karimas'** (*kariru, karite*) 借りる
bosom **futokoro** ふところ
boss **shujin** 主人
both **ryōhō** 両方 *or* **dochira mo** どちらも
bother **mendō** 面倒 *or* **meiwaku** 迷惑
bothersome **mendō-kusai** 面倒臭い
bottle **bin** びん
bottle opener **sennuki** 栓抜き
bottom **soko** 底 「はずむ
bounce **hazumimas'** (*hazumu, hazunde*)
bound (for) **. . . e ikimas'** (*iku, itte*) へ行く

bound (to) **kitto ... (suru) deshō** きっと…(する)でしょう
bouquet **hanataba** 花束
bourbon **burubon** ブルボン
bow (*of head, etc.*) **ojigi (o shimas'**; *suru, sh'te*) お辞儀(をする)
bow (*shooting or violin*) **yumi** 弓
bowel movement **daiben (shimas'**; *suru, sh'te*) 大便(する)
bowl **chawan** 茶碗
bowl(ful) **-hai** 杯 (1 **ip-pai**, 2 **ni-hai**, 3 **sam-bai**)
bowlegged **gani-mata** がにまた *or* **wani-ashi** わに足
box **hako** 箱
boxing **kentō** 拳闘 *or* **bokkushingu** ボックシング
box office **kippu uriba** 切符売り場
boxtree **tsuge** つげ
boy **kodomo** 子供 *or* **otoko no ko** 男の子 *or* **bōya** 坊や *or* **botchan** 坊ちゃん
bracelet **ude-wa** 腕輪
brag about **jiman shimas'** (*suru, sh'te*) 自慢する *or* **hokorimas'** (*hokoru, hokotte*) 誇る
braid **amimas'** (*amu, ande*) 編む
brains **nō-miso** 脳味噌 *or* **atama** 頭
brakes **burēki** ブレーキ *or* **wa-dome** 輪止め
branch (*of tree*) **eda** 枝; (*of store*) **shi-ten** 支店; (*of rail line*) **shi-sen** 支線
brass **shinchū** 真鍮
brassiere **burajia** ブラジア *or* **burā** ブラー
brave **yūkan (na)** 勇敢(な)
brazier **hibachi** 火鉢

Brazil **Burajiru** ブラジル
bread **pan** パン *or* **shoku-pan** 食パン
bread crumbs **pan-ko** パン粉
break (*it breaks*) **kowaremas'** (*kowareru, kowarete*) こわれる; (*breaks it*) **kowashimas'** (*kowasu, kowash'te*) こわす
breakable **koware-yasui** こわれやすい
breakfast **asa-han** 朝飯
(sea) bream **tai** たい
breast (*chest*) **mune** 胸; (*woman's*) **chichi** 乳
breathe **iki o shimas'** (*suru, sh'te*) 息をする
breechcloth **fundoshi** ふんどし
breeches *see* trousers
breeze *see* wind
brewery **jōzōsho** 醸造所
bribe **wairo** わいろ
brick **renga** 煉瓦
bride **hana-yome** 花嫁
bridegroom **hana-muko** 花婿
bridge **hashi** 橋
bridle **baroku** 馬勒
brief *see* short
brief case **kaban** かばん
brigade **ryodan** 旅団
brigadier general **dai-shō** 代将 *or* **jun-shō** 準将
bright **akarui** 明るい
bring (*a thing*) **motte kimas'** (*kuru, kite*) 持つて来る; (*a person*) **tsurete kimas'** (*kuru, kite*) 連れて来る

Britain *see* England
British *see* English
brittle **moroi** 脆い
broad *see* wide
broadcast **hōsō (shimas'**; *suru, sh'te*) 放送(する)
broadcasting station **hōsō-kyoku** 放送局
brocade **nishiki** 錦
broil **yakimas'** (*yaku, yaite*) 燒く
broken (*not working*) **dame des'** だめです *or* **koshō shimash'ta** 故障しました
brokenhearted **shitsuren** 失恋
broker **naka-gai** 仲買 *or* **naka-dachi** 仲立
brook **ogawa** 小川
broom **hōki** 帚
bronze **seidō** 青銅
brothel **jorō-ya** 女郎屋
brother **otoko no kyōdai** 男のきょうだい; (*older brother*) **nii-san** 兄さん *or* **ani** 兄; (*younger brother*) **otōto (san)** 弟(さん)
brow (*eyebrow*) **mayu** まゆ; (*forehead*) **hitai** ひたい
brown **cha-iro (no)** 茶色(の)
brown bread **kuro-pan** 黒パン
bruise **uchi-kizu** 打ちきず
brush **burashi** ブラシ *or* **hake** はけ; (*for writing or painting*) **fude** 筆
Brussels sprouts **me-kyabetsu** 芽キャベツ
brutal **zankoku (na)** 残酷(な)
bubble **awa** 泡 *or* **abuku** あぶく; (*soap*) **shabon-dama** シャボン玉

bubble gum **fūsen-gamu** 風船ガム
bucket **baketsu** バケツ *or* **oke** 桶
buckle **shime-gane** 締金
buck private **heisotsu** 兵卒
bucktooth **soppa** 反歯
buckwheat (noodles) **(o-)soba** (お)そば
bud *(of leaf)* **me** 芽; *(of flower)* **tsubomi** 蕾
Buddha **Hotoke-sama** 仏様; *(statue of)* **Butsu-zō** 仏像
Buddhism **Bukkyō** 仏教
Buddhist priest **bōzu** 坊主 *or* **sōryo** 僧侶
Buddhist temple **(o-)tera** (お)寺
buddy *see* friend
budge *see* move
budget **yosan** 予算
bug **mushi** 虫
bugle **rappa** らっぱ
build **tatemas'** *(tateru, tatete)* 建てる
building **tatemono** 建物 *or* **birujingu** ビルジング
(light) bulb **denkyū** 電球
bulge **fukurami** 脹らみ
(in) bulk **bara de** ばらで
bulldozer **burudōza** ブルドーザ *or* **ji-narashi** 地均し
bullet **tama** たま *or* **dangan** 弾丸
bulletin board **keiji-ban** 掲示板
bum **rumpen** ルンペン
bump (into) **. . . ni butsukarimas'** *(butsukaru, butsukatte)* にぶつかる
bump *(swelling)* **kobu** 瘤; *(in road)* **dekoboko** でこぼこ
bunch *(cluster)* **fusa** 房; *(pile)* **yama** 山;

(*bundle*) **taba** 束; (*group*) **mure** 群
bundle **tsutsumi** 包み
bunion **soko-mame** 底豆
bureau (*department*) **kyoku** 局; (*chest*) **tansu** 「たんす
burglar **dorobō** 泥棒
burlesque **s'torippu** ストリップ
Burma **Biruma** ビルマ
burn (*it burns up*) **yakemas'** (*yakeru, yakete*) 焼ける; (*burns it up*) **yakimas'** (*yaku, yaite*) 焼く; (*fire burns*) **moemas'** (*moeru, moete*) 燃える
burp **geppu** (**o dashimas'**; *dasu, dash'te*) 「げっぷ(を出す)
burst (*it bursts*) **yaburemas'** (*yabureru, yaburete*) 破れる; (*bursts it*) **yaburimas'** (*yaburu, yabutte*) 破る
bury **umemas'** (*umeru, umete*) 埋める
bus **basu** バス
bush **kamboku** 灌木
business (*job*) **shigoto** 仕事
business (*enterprise*) **jitsugyō** 実業; (*commerce*) **shōgyō** 商業
business (*errand, etc.*) **yō** 用 *or* **yōji** 用事
businessman **jitsugyōka** 実業家
bust *see* burst
busy **isogashii** 忙しい
but **sh'kashi** しかし *or* **keredomo** けれども *or* **...** (**des'**) **ga** です(が)
butcher (shop) **niku-ya** 肉屋
butt (*cigarette*) **suigara** 吸い殻

butter **batā** バター
butterfly **chō** *or* **chōchō** 蝶(々)
buttocks **shiri** 尻　「ボタン(をかける)
button **botan** (**o kakemas'**; *kakeru, kakete*)
buy **kaimas'** (*kau, katte*) 買う
by (*not later than*) **...made ni** までに
by means of **...de** で

C

cab *see* taxi
cabaret **kyabarē** キャバレー
cabbage **kyabetsu** キャベツ
cable (**kaigai**) **dempō** (海外)電報
cactus **saboten** さぼてん
cafe (*coffee shop*) **kōhii-ten** コーヒー店; (*restaurant*) **ryōri-ten** 料理店
cage (*for birds*) **kago** 籠; (*for animals*) **ori** 檻
cake **kēki** ケーキ; (*Japanese*) **o-kashi** お菓子; (spongecake) **kas'tera** カステラ
calamity **sainan** 災難
calendar **koyomi** 暦
calisthenics **taisō** 体操
call **yobimas'** (*yobu, yonde*) 呼ぶ
calligraphy **shodō** 書道
calling card **meishi** 名刺
calling-card case **meishi-ire** 名刺入れ
callus **tako** たこ　「平気で
calm(ly) **ochitsuite** おちついて *or* **heiki de**

camel **rakuda** らくだ
camera **shashinki** 写真機
camp **kyampu** キャンプ
campus **kōtei** 校庭
can (*tin*) **kan** 鑵
can (*is able*) **dekimas'** (***dekiru, dekite***) 出来る; (**suru**) **koto ga dekimas'** (する)事が出來る
Canada **Kanada** カナダ
Canadian **Kanada-jin** カナダ人
canary **kanariya** カナリヤ
cancel (**tori-**)**keshimas'** (***kesu, kesh'te***)(取)消す
cancer **gan** がん
candle **rōsoku** ろうそく
candy **o-kashi** お菓子
candy store **kashi-ya** 菓子屋
cane **s'tekki** ステッキ
canned goods **kanzume** 鑵詰
cannon **taihō** 大砲
can opener **kan-kiri** 鑵切り
canvas (*material*) **zukku** ズック
cap *see* hat
cape (of land) **misaki** 岬
capital (city) **shufu** 首府
capital (*money*) **shihon** 資本
capitalism **shihon-shugi** 資本主義
capitalist **shihon-ka** 資本家
capsule **kapuseru** カプセル
captain (*army*) **tai-i** 大尉; (*navy*) **tai-sa** 大佐
car **kuruma** 車; **jidōsha** 自動車

caramel **kyarameru** キャラメル

carbarn **shako** 車庫

carbolic acid **sekitan-san** 石炭酸

cardboard **bōru-gami** ボール紙

cards **torampu** トランプ

care **yōjin** 用心

career **shokugyō** 職業

(is) careful **ki o ts'kemas'** (*ts'keru, ts'kete*) 気を付ける

carp (*fish*) **koi** 鯉

carpenter **daiku** 大工

carpet **jūtan** *or* **kāpetto** カーペット

carrot **ninjin** 人参

carry **motte ikimas'** (*iku, itte*) 持って行く

(hand)cart **te-guruma** 手車 *or* **kuruma** 車

carton *see* box

cartoon **manga** 漫画

carve **kizamimas'** (*kizamu, kizande*) 刻む *or* **horimas'** (*horu, hotte*) 彫る

carving **horimono** 彫物

case (*circumstance*) **ba(w)ai** 場合; (*box*) **hako** 箱

cash (on hand) **gen-nama** 現なま

cash (a check, etc.) **genkin ni hiki-kaemas'** (*-kaeru, -kaete*) 現金に引換える

cash (a large bill) **komakaku shimas'** (*suru, sh'te*) 細かくする

cashbox **kane-bako** 金箱

cashier **kanjō-gakari** 勘定係

cask **taru** 樽

cast (*of play*) **yakuwari** 役割り

castle **(o-)shiro** (お)城

casual **nanige-nai** 何げない
cat **neko** 猫 「名簿
catalog **mokuroku** 目録; (*directory*) **meibo**
catch **torimas'** (*toru, totte*) 取る
caterpillar **kemushi** 毛虫
catfish **namazu** なまず
Catholic **Katorikku** カトリック
cattle **ushi** 牛
cause (*of an effect*) **moto** 元 *or* **gen-in** 原因; (*reason*) **wake** わけ *or* **riyū** 理由; (*purpose*) **tame** 為 「*seru, sasete*) にさせる
cause (someone to do) **...ni sasemas'** (*sa-*
cautious **yōjim-bukai** 用心深い
cave **hora(-ana)** ほら(穴)
cedar **sugi** 杉
ceiling **tenjō** 天井
celebrate **iwaimas'** (*iwau, iwatte*) 祝う
celery **serori** セロリ
cellar **chika-shitsu** 地下室
cement **semento** セメント
cemetery **hakaba** 墓場 *or* **bochi** 墓地
censor(ship) **ken-etsu** 検閲
cent **sento** セント
center **mannaka** まん中
centimeter **senchi(-mētoru)** センチ(メートル)
centipede **mukade** むかで
century **hyaku-nen** 百年 *or* **seiki** 世紀
ceremony **shiki** 式
certain **tash'ka (na)** 確か(な)

certainly **mochiron** 勿論 「下水だめ
cesspool **osui-dame** 汚水だめ *or* **gesui-dame**
Ceylon **Seiron** セイロン
chain **kusari** 鎖(くさり)
chair **isu** 椅子
chalk **chōku** チョーク
chance **chansu** チャンス
change (*it changes*) **kawarimas'** (*kawaru, kawatte*) 変る; (*changes it*) **kaemas'** (*kaeru, kaete*) 変える (換える, 替える); (*changes trains, etc.*) **nori-kaemas'** (*-kaeru, kaete*) 乗り換える
change (*small money*) **komakai** (**kane**) こまかい(金); (*money returned*) **o-tsuri** お釣
character (*quality*) **seishitsu** 性質; (*personal*
charcoal **sumi** 炭 ⌊*traits*) **seikaku** 性格
charcoal brazier *see* brazier
charge (how much) (**ikura**) **shimas'** (*suru,*
charity **hodokoshi** 施し ⌊*sh'te*) いくらする
charm (*good-luck piece*) **o-mamori** お守り
(is) charming **miryoku ga arimas'** (*aru, atte*) 魅力がある 「かける
chase **oi-kakemas'** (*-kakeru, -kakete*) 追い
chaser **ato-nomi** 後飲
chaste **teisetsu** (**na**) 貞節(な) 「立話
chat **sekem-banashi** 世間話 *or* **tachi-banashi**
chatter **shaberimas'** (*shaberu, shabette*) 喋る
chatterbox **oshaberi** おしゃべり
chauffeur **untenshu** 運転手

cheap **yasui** 安い
cheat **damashimas'** (*damasu, damash'te*) 「だます
check (*bank*) **kogitte** 小切手; (*baggage*) **chikki** チッキ
checkers (*Japanese*) **go** 碁
checkroom **azukari-jo** 預り所
cheek **hoppeta** ほっぺた
cheerful **kigen ga ii** 機嫌がいい
cheese **chiizu** チーズ
cheesecloth **kanreisha** かんれいしゃ
chef *see* cook
chemistry **kagaku** *or* **bake-gaku** 化学
cherry (tree) **sakura** さくら (桜); (*fruit*) **sakurambo** さんらんぼ
cherry blossoms **sakura no hana** さくらの花
chest (*of body*) **mune** 胸; (of drawers) **tansu** たんす
chestnut **kuri** くり (栗); (*roasted*) **yaki-guri** 「焼ぐり
chew **kamimas'** (*kamu, kande*) かむ
chicken **tori** 鳥 *or* **niwatori** 鶏
chief (*head*) **chō** 長 *or* **chōkan** 長官; (*principal*) **shuyō (na)** 主要(な) *or* **omo (na)** 主(な)
child **kodomo** 子供 *or* **ko** 子
childhood **kodomo no toki** 子供の時
chill(y) *see* cold
chimney **entotsu** 煙突
chin **ago** あご
China **Chūgoku** 中国
Chinese (*person*) **Chūgoku-jin** 中国人
Chinese character **kanji** 漢字

chip (*of wood*) **koppa** こっぱ; (*crack*) **kizu** きず
chisel **nomi** のみ
chlorine **enso** 塩素
chocolate **chokorēto** チョコレート
chocolate malt **choko-moruto** チョコモルト
chocolate milk **choko-miruku** チョコミルク
choir **kōrasu** コーラス
choke (*he chokes*) **iki ga tsumarimas'** (*tsumaru, tsumatte*) 息が詰る; (*chokes him*) **...no iki o tomemas'** (*tomeru, tomete*)
cholera **korera** コレラ ⌊の息を止める
choose **erabimas'** (*erabu, erande*) 選ぶ
chop *see* cut
chopping board **manaita** まないた
chopstick rest **hashi-oki** 箸置き
chopsticks **o-hashi** お箸
chow *see* food
chow mein **yaki-soba** 焼そば
Christ **Kiris'to** キリスト
Christianity **Kiris'to-kyō** キリスト教
Christmas **Kurisumas'** クリスマス
chrysanthemum **kiku** きく(菊)
church **kyōkai** 教会 ⌈*soda pop*)
"cider" **saidā** サイダー (*a very fizzy lemon*
cigar **shigā** シガー *or* **hamaki** 葉巻
cigarette case **tabako-ire** たばこ入れ ⌈吸口
cigarette holder **paipu** パイプ *or* **suikuchi**
cigarettes **tabako** たばこ
cinch **wake mo nai (koto)** 訳もない(事)

cinder **moegara** 燃がら
cinema *see* movies
cinnamon **nikkei** 肉桂
circle **maru** 丸 *or* **en** 円
circulate (*it circulates*) **mawarimas'** (*mawaru, mawatte*) 廻る; (*circulates it*) **mawashimas'** (*mawasu, mawash'te*) 廻す
circumstance **ba(w)ai** 場合 *or* **koto** 事
circus **sākasu** サーカス *or* **kyokuba** 曲馬
city **machi** 町
civilian **shimin** 市民 「**heijō-f'ku** 平常服
civilian clothes, civies **fudan-gi** 不断着 *or*
civilization **bummei** 文明 *or* **bunka** 文化
clan **uji** 氏 「手をたたく
clap (hands) **te o tatakimas'** (*tataku, tataite*)
class **kurasu** クラス *or* **kyū** 級
classroom **kyōshitsu** 教室 「はさみ
claw (*of animal*) **tsume** 爪; (*of crab*) **hasami**
claw hammer **kuginuki** 釘抜き
clay **nendo** 粘土
clean **kirei** (**na**) きれい (な); (*cleans it*) **sōji shimas'** (*suru, sh'te*) 掃除する 「リーニング
cleaning (*dry*) **dorai-kuaiiningu** ドライ・ク
clear (*bright*) **akarui** 明るい; (*understood*) **wakatta** 解った; (*easy to see*) **mi-yasui** 見やすい; (*easy to understand*) **wakari-yasui** 解りやすい; (*unimpeded*) **jama ga nai** じゃまがない
clearly (*distinctly*) **hakkiri** はっきり

clerk (*in shop*) **ten-in** 店員; (*in office*) **jimu-in** 事務員
clever **rikō** (**na**) 利口(な)
cliff **gake** 崖
climate **kikō** 気候
climb **noborimas'** (*noboru, nobotte*) 上る
clippers (*barber's*) **barikan** バリカン
clock **tokei** 時計
clockwise **migi-mawari** (**ni**) 右廻りに
clogs *see* wooden shoes
close **shimemas'** (*shimeru, shimete*) 締める
close *see* near
closet **oshi-ire** 押入れ
cloth **orimono** 織物; (a piece of) **kire** きれ
clothes **kimono** 着物; (American) **yōf'ku** 洋服; (Japanese) **waf'ku** 和服
clothesbag **sentaku-ire** 洗濯入れ
clothesbrush **kimono-burashi** 着物ブラシ
clothesline **mono-hoshi** 物干し
cloud **kumo** 雲
(gets) cloudy **kumorimas'** (*kumoru, kumotte*) 曇る
cloves **chōji** 丁子
club (*social group or card suit*) **kurabu** クラブ; (*stick*) **kombō** 棍棒; (*golf club*) **uchi-bō** 打棒
clue **itoguchi** いとぐち
clumsy **heta** (**na**) 下手 (な) *or* **bukiyō** (**na**) 不器用(な)
cluster *see* bunch
coach (*railroad*) **kyaku-sha** 客車; (*athletic*) **kōchi** コーチ
coal **sekitan** 石炭
coal mine **tankō** 炭坑

coast **kaigan** 海岸
coat **uwagi** 上着; (overcoat) **gaitō** 外套
coax **odatemas'** (*odateru, odatete*) おだてる
cobweb **kumo no su** (*or* **ito**) くもの巣(糸)
cockroach **abura-mushi** 油虫
cocktail (party) **kakuteru** カクテル
cocoa **kokoa** ココア
coconut **yashi** やし
cocoon **mayu** まゆ
cod(fish) **tara** 鱈
co-ed **mech'-kō** メチ公 *or* **jogak'sei** 女学生
co-existence **kyōzon** 共存
coffee **kōhii** コーヒー
coffeehouse **kōhii-ten** コーヒー店
coffee cup **kōhii-jawan** コーヒー茶碗
coin **tama** 玉 *or* **kōka** 硬貨; (*brass or copper*) **dōka** 銅貨; (10 Yen) **jū-en-dama;** (5 Yen) **go-en-dama** 十(五)円玉
colander **mizu-koshi** 水こし
cold **samui** 寒い; (*to the touch*) **tsumetai** 「冷い
(catches) cold **kaze o hikimas'** (*hiku, hiite*) 風邪を引く
coleslaw **kyabetsu-sarada** キャベツ・サラダ
collapse **tsuburemas'** (*tsubureru, tsuburete*) つぶれる
collar (*of coat*) **eri** えり; (*of dog*) **kubi-wa** 首輪
collect (*collects them*) **atsumemas'** (*atsumeru, atsumete*) 集める; (*they collect*) **atsumarimas'** (*atsumaru, atsumatte*) 集まる

college **daigaku** 大学
collision **shōtotsu** 衝突
colloquial (language) **kōgo** 口語
colonel **taisa** 大佐
colony **shokumin-chi** 植民地
color **iro** 色
comb **kushi** くし (櫛)
comb (the hair) **kami o tokashimas'** (*tokasu, tokash'te*) 髪をとかす
combination **kumi-awase** 組合せ
combine **awasemas'** (*awaseru, awasete*) 合せる
come **kimas'** (*kuru, kite*) 来る
comet **hōki-boshi** ほうき星
comfortable **raku (na)** 楽(な)
comic book **manga-bon** 漫画本
comics **manga** 漫画
command **. . . ni ii-ts'kemas'** (*-ts'keru, -ts'kete*) に言い付ける
commander (*navy*) 中佐 **chūsa**
commerce **shōgyō** 商業
committee **iinkai** 委員会
common **futsū (no)** 普通(の)
Communism **Kyōsan-shugi** 共産主義
community **shakai** 社会
commute **kayoimas'** (*kayou, kayotte*) 通う
commuter's ticket **teiki (ken)** 定期(券)
companion *see* friend
company (*firm*) **kaisha** 会社
compare **kurabemas'** (*kuraberu, kurabete*) 比べる
compass (*for directions*) **rashimban** 羅針盤;

(*for drafting*) **kompasu** コンパス
complaint **fuhei** 不平 *or* **kogoto** 小言
completely **zembu** 全部 *or* **minna** 皆
complicated **fukuzatsu (na)** 複雑 (な) *or* **komi-itta** 込み入った
compliment **o-seji** お世辞
compromise **dakyō** 妥協
comrade **dōshi** 同志
conceal *see* hide
concert **ongakkai** 音楽会
condition (*state*) **arisama** 有様 *or* **jōtai** 状態; (*stipulation*) **jōken** 条件
condom **sakku** サック
conductor (*train, etc.*) **shashō (san)** 車掌(さん)
conference **sōdan** 相談; (*formal*) **kaigi** 会議
confess **uchi-akemas'** (*-akeru, -akete*) 打ち明ける
confidence **shin-yō** 信用; (self-) **jishin** 自信
confidential *see* secret
Confucianism **Jukyō** 儒教
Confucius **Kōshi** 孔子
confused **komarimas'** (*komaru, komatte*) 困る
Congratulations! **Omedetō gozaimas'.** おめでとうございます
conjunction **setsuzoku-shi** 接続詞
(it) connects (with) **. . . to renraku shimas'** (*suru, sh'te*) と連絡する 「関係
connection **renraku** 連絡; (*relevance*) **kankei**
conscience **ryōshin** 良心

conscientious **majime (na)** まじめ(な)
consent **shōchi shimas'** (*suru, sh'te*) 承知する
consequence *see* result
consider **kangaemas'** (*kangaeru, kangaete*) 考える
considerable **sōtō** 相当
consideration (*being kind*) **omoiyari** おもいやり
consonant **shiin** *or* **shion** 子音
constantly *see* always
constipation **bempi** 便秘
construction (work) **kōji** 工事
consul **ryōji** 領事
consulate **ryōji-kan** 領事館
contact (*a person*) **. . . to renraku shimas'** (*suru, sh'te*) と連絡する *or* **. . . ni aimas'** (*au, atte*) に合う
contain **. . . ga haitte imas'** (*iru, ite*) がはいっている
contented (with) **. . . de manzoku shimas'** (*suru, sh'te*) で満足する
contest **konkūru** コンクール
continent **tairiku** 大陸
continue (*it continues*) **tsuzukimas'** (*tsuzuku, tsuzuite*) 続く; (*continues it*) **tsuzukemas'** (*tsuzukeru, tsuzukete*) 続ける
contract **keiyaku** 契約
contradiction (*inconsistency*) **mujun** 矛盾
control (*supervise*) **tori-shimarimas'** (*-shimaru, -shimatte*) 取締る
convenient **benri (na)** 便利な
convent **shūdōin** 修道院

conversation (*ordinary*) **hanashi** 話; (*in language class, etc.*) **kaiwa** 会話
converter **henkanki** 変換器; (*AC-DC*) **henryūki** 変流機; (*transformer*) **hen-ats'ki** 変圧機
cook **kokku (san)** コック(さん); (*cooks it*) **ryōri shimas'** (*suru, sh'te*) 料理する
cool **suzushii** 涼しい
cooperation **kyōryoku** 協力
copper **aka-gane** *or* **dō** 銅 「" it is," *etc.*)
copula **shitei-shi** 指定詞 (*the word* **des'**
copy (**ichi-**)**bu** (一)部 「*utsush'te*) 写す
copy (*makes a . . .*) **utsushimas'** (*utsusu,*
coral **sango** さんご
cord **himo** ひも
core **shin** 心
corkscrew **koruku-nuki** コルク抜き
corn **tō-morokoshi** とうもろこし 「**sumi** すみ
corner (*outside*) **kado** かど (角); (*inside*)
corporal **gochō** 伍長
corps **gundan** 軍団 「死人
corpse **shitai** 死体 *or* **shigai** 死骸 *or* **shinin**
correct **tadashii** 正しい
correspondence **tsūshin** 通信
corridor **rōka** 廊下
corrugated cardboard **dam-boru** 段ボール
cosmetics **keshō-hin** 化粧品
cost (how much) (**ikura**) **shimas'** (*suru,*
cotton **wata** わた (綿) ⌊*sh'te*) (いくら) する
cough **seki o shimas'** (*suru, sh'te*) 咳をする

could *see* can
count **kazoemas'** (*kazoeru, kazoete*) 数える
counterclockwise **hidari-mawari (ni)** 左廻り(に)
country (*nation*) **kuni** 国; (*farm*) **inaka** 田舎
county **gun** 郡
couple *see* two
course (*in school*) **kamoku** 科目
court (*law*) **saiban** 裁判
cousin **itoko** いとこ
cover (*lid*) **futa** ふた
cow **ushi** 牛
crab **kani** かに
crack (*wide*) **ware-me** 割れ目; (*fine*) **hibi** ひび
crackers **kurakkā** クラッカー *or* **bis'ketto** ビスケット
cradle **yuri-kago** ゆりかご
crater **funka-kō** 噴火口
crazy **ki-chigai (no)** 気違い(の)
cream **kuriimu** クリーム
crime **tsumi** 罪 *or* **hanzai** 犯罪「**fugu** 不具
cripple **katawa** 片輪 *or* **chimba** ちんば *or*
crock **tsubo** つぼ
crossing (*street intersection*) **kōsaten** 交叉点
crotch **mata** また
crow **karasu** からす
crowded **konde imas'** (*iru, ite*) こんでいる
cruel **zankoku (na)** 残酷(な)
crush (*crushes it*) **tsubushimas'** (*tsubusu, tsubush'te*) つぶす; (*it crushes*) **tsubure-**

mas' (*tsubureru, tsuburete*) つぶれる
crust **kawa** 皮
crutches **matsuba-zue** 松葉杖
cry **nakimas'** (*naku, naite*) 泣く
cuckoo **hototogisu** ほととぎす
cucumber **kyūri** きゅうり
culture (*refinement*) **kyōyō** 教養; (*civilization*) **bunka** 文化
cup **chawan** 茶碗; (*a . . . of*) ip-pai 一杯
cupboard **shokki-dana** 食器棚
cure **naoshimas'** (*naosu, naosh'te*) 直す
(gets) cured **naorimas'** (*naoru, naotte*) 直る
curios **kottō-hin** こっとう品
curious **monozuki** (na) 物好き(な)
curry **karē** カレー; (*with rice*) **karē-raisu** カレー・ライス
curtains **kāten** カーテン *or* **mado-kake** 窓掛
cushion (*seat*) **zabuton** 座ぶとん
custom **shūkan** 習慣
customer **kyaku** 客; **o-kyaku san** お客さん
customs **kanzei** 関税
cut **kirimas'** (*kiru, kitte*) 切る
cute **kawaii** かわいい
cuttlefish (*squid*) **ika** いか
cypress **hinoki** ひのき

D

dairy **gyūnyū-ya** 牛乳屋 *or* **miruku-ten** ミルク店
dam **damu** ダム

damascene **nie** にえ
damask **donsu** どんす
damp **shimeppoi** しめっぽい 「(をする)
dance **odori (o shimas'**; *suru, sh'te*) 踊り
dandruff **fuke** ふけ
danger **kiken** 危険
dangerous **abunai** 危い
dark **kurai** 暗い
date (*engagement*) **yakusoku** 約束
date (*a couple*) **abekku** アベック
date (*of month*) **hizuke** 日付け
daughter **musume (san)** むすめ(さん)
dawn **yoake** 夜明け
day **hi** 日; (*daytime*) **hiru (ma)** 昼(間)
day after tomorrow **asatte** あさって
day before yesterday **ototoi** おととい
D.C. (current) **chokuryū** 直流
dead **shinde imas'** (*iru, ite*) 死んでいる
deaf **tsumbo (no)** つんぼ(の)
debt **shakkin** 借金
deceive *see* cheat
December **Jūni-gatsu** 十二月
decide **kimemas'** (*kimeru, kimete*) 定める
decline (*refuse*) **kotowarimas'** (*kotowaru,*
deep **fukai** 深い ⌊*kotowatte*) ことわる
deer **sh'ka** 鹿 「負かす
defeat **makashimas'** (*makasu, makash'te*)
defend **mamorimas'** (*mamoru, mamotte*) 守る
degree (*extent*) **teido** 程度

(is) delayed **okuremas'** (*okureru, okurete*)
遅れる 「わざわざ
deliberately **waza to** わざと; **waza-waza**
delicious **oishii** おいしい *or* **umai** うまい
delightful **ureshii** うれしい 「届ける
deliver **todokemas'** (*todokeru, todokete*)
demand **motomemas'** (*motomeru, motomete*)
democracy **minshu-shugi** 民主主義 ∟求める
dentist **ha-isha** 歯医者
deny **uchi-keshimas'** (*-kesu, -kesh'te*) 打消す
deodorant **shūki-dome** 臭気止め
department store **depāto** デパート
depilatory **datsumō-zai** 脱毛剤
deposit **azukemas'** (*azukeru, azukete*) 預ける
depressed (*feeling*) **ki ga omoi** 気が重い
depression (*hard times*) **fukeiki** 不景気
describe **. . . (no koto o) kuwashiku iimas'**
(*yū, yutte* or *itte*) (の事を) 詳しく言う
description **setsumei** 説明
desert **sabaku** さばく (砂漠) 「欲しい
desirable **nozomashii** 望ましい *or* **hoshii**
desire **hoshii** ほしい
desk **ts'kue** つくえ (机)
desperately **isshō-kemmei ni** 一生懸命に
dessert **dezāto** デザート 「こわす
destroy **kowashimas'** (*kowasu, kowash'te*)
detailed **kuwashii** 詳しい
detective **tantei** 探偵
detour **mawari-michi** 回り路 *or* **ukai** 迂回

or **tōmawari** 遠回り
device **kufū** 工夫; (*gadget*) **shikake** 仕掛け
devil **oni** 鬼
dew **tsuyu** つゆ(露)
diabetes **tōnyō-byō** 糖尿病
dialect **namari** 訛り *or* **hōgen** 方言
diapers **oshime** おしめ *or* **omutsu** おむつ
diarrhea **geri** 下痢
diary **nikki** 日記
dictation **kakitori** 書き取り
dictator **wam-man** ワンマン
dictionary **jibiki** 字引
did *see* do
die **shinimas'** (*shinu, shinde*) 死ぬ *or* **naku-narimas'** (*-naru, -natte*) なくなる
Diet (*parliament*) **Kokkai** 国会 *or* **Gikai** 議会
different **chigaimas'** (*chigau, chigatte*) 違う
difficult **muzukashii** むづかしい
dig **horimas'** (*horu, hotte*) 掘る
digest **konashimas'** (*konasu, konash'te*) こなす
dike **tsutsumi** 堤 *or* **dote** 土手
dimple **ekubo** えくぼ
diner (*on train*) **shokudō-sha** 食堂車
dining room **shokudō** 食堂
dinner **shokuji** 食事 *or* **gohan** 御飯
diplomat **gaikōkan** 外交官
direct **chokusetsu** 直接
direction **hō** 方 *or* **hōkō** 方向
directory (*telephone*) **denwa-chō** 電話帳

dirt **doro** 泥
dirty **kitanai** きたない 「がっかりする
disappointed **gakkari shimas'** (*suru, sh'te*)
discount **wari-biki** 割引
discourtesy **burei** 無礼 *or* **shitsurei** 失礼
discover **mi-tsukemas'** (*-tsukeru, -tsukete*)
disease **byōki** 病気 ⌊見つける
disgraceful **hazukashii** はずかしい
disgusting **iya (na)** いや(な)
dish **sara** 皿
dishpan **sara-arai-oke** 皿洗い桶
disinfectant **shōdoku-zai** 消毒剤
dislike **...ga kirai des'** がきらいです
dispensary **yakkyoku** 薬局 「態度
disposition **seishitsu** 性質; (*attitude*) **taido**
dissipation **dōraku** 道楽
dissolve (*dissolves it*) **tokashimas'** (*tokasu, tokash'te*) 溶かす; (*it dissolves*) **tokemas'**
distance **kyori** 距離 ⌊(*tokeru, tokete*) 溶ける
distant *see* far
distinctly **hakkiri** はっきり
distress **nayami** 悩み
distribute **kubarimas'** (*kubaru, kubatte*) 配る
district **chihō** 地方 「をする
disturb **jama o shimas'** (*suru, sh'te*) じゃま
ditch **mizo** 溝
divide (*divides it*) **wakemas'** (*wakeru, wakete*) 分ける; (*it divides*) **wakaremas'** (*wakareru,*
divorce **rikon** 離婚 ⌊*wakarete*) 分れる

do **shimas'** (*suru, sh'te*) する
dock **dokku** ドック
doctor **(o-)isha (san)** お医者(さん)
Dr . . . **. . . sensei** 先生
dog **inu** 犬
doll **ningyō** 人形
Doll Festival **Hina-matsuri** 雛祭
dollar **doru** ドル
done (*ready*) **dekimash'ta** 出來ました *or* **dekite imas'** (*iru, ite*) 出来ている, (*finished*) **. . . te shimaimash'ta** (*shimatta, shimatte*) . . . てしまった
(half-)done (*medium*) **han-yake no** 半燒けの
(under) done (*rare*) **nama-yake no** 生燒けの
(well-)done **yoku yaketa** よく燒けた
donkey **roba** ろば
Don't! **Dame des'!** だめです
door **to** 戸
dope **mayaku** 麻薬
dormitory **kishuk'sha** 寄宿舎
dot **ten** 点
double **bai (no)** 倍(の)
double-cross **ura-giri** 裏切
doubt **utagaimas'** (*utagau, utagatte*) 疑う
douche **chūsui-ki** 注水器
dough **neri-ko** 練粉 *or* **nama-pan** 生パン
dove **hato** はと
down **shita e** 下へ
(gets) down **orimas'** (*oriru, orite*) 下りる

(one) dozen **(ichi-)dāsu** (1) ダース *or* **jū ni**十二
drag **hipparimas'** *(hipparu, hippatte)* 引っぱる
dragon **ryū** 竜
drain *(kitchen)* **gesui** 下水
dramamine **doramamin** ドラマミン
drapes **kāten** カーテン
draw (a picture) **egakimas'** *(egaku, egaite)* 描く
drawer *(of desk, etc.)* **hiki-dashi** 引出し
drawers *(underwear)* **zubon-sh'ta** ズボン下
dreadful **osoroshii** 恐ろしい
dream **yume (o mimas'**; *miru, mite)* 夢(を見る)
dress **kimono (o kimas'**; *kiru, kite)* 着物(を着る)
dressmaker **yōsai(-shi)** 洋裁師 *or* **doresu-mēka** ドレス・メーカ
drink **nomimas'** *(nomu, nonde)* 飲む
drinking water **nomi-mizu** 飲水
drive (a car) **unten shimas'** *(suru, sh'te)* 運転する
drive-in **nori-komi** 乗り込み
driver **unten-shu** 運転手
driveway **shadō** 車道
drop **otoshimas'** *(otosu, otosh'te)* 落す
drown **obore-jini shimas'** *(suru, sh'te)* 溺れ死にする
drug **k'suri** 薬
drugstore **k'suri-ya** 薬屋
drum **taiko** 太鼓; *(hourglass-shaped)* **tsuzumi** 鼓
(gets) drunk **yopparaimas'** *(yopparau, yopparatte)* よっぱらう
dry *(it dries)* **kawakimas'** *(kawaku, kawaite)* 乾く; *(dries it)* **kawakashimas'** *(kawa-*

kasu, kawakash'te) 乾かす 「ニング
dry cleaning **dorai-kuriiningu** ドライ・クリー
duck (*wild*) **kamo** 鴨; (*tame*) **ahiru** あひる
due to *see* because; *see* supposed to
dull **nibui** 鈍い; (*uninteresting*) **taikutsu (na)** 退屈(な)
dumpling (*large meat-stuffed*) **manjū** まんじゅう; (*small meat-stuffed*) **gyōza** ぎょうざ
dung **k'so** 糞
during (**. . . no**) **aida** (の)間
dust (*on ground*) **chiri** ちり; (*in air*) **hokori** ほこり; (*in house*) **gomi** ごみ
dust pan **chiri tori** チリ取り
Dutch **Oranda(-jin)** オランダ(人)
(going) Dutch **wari-kan** 割勘
duty **gimu** 義務 *or* **hombun** 本分
(is on) duty **tōban (des')** 当番(です)
duty (*import*) **yunyūzei** 輸入税; *see also* customs
dwarf trees **bonsai** 盆栽
dwindle **herimas'** (*heru, hette*) 減る *or* **chiisaku narimas'** (*naru, natte*) 小さくなる
dye **somemas'** (*someru, somete*) 染める

E

each **. . . zutsu** ずつ
eagerly **nesshin ni** 熱心に
eagle **washi** わし
ear **mimi** 耳

early hayai (hayaku) 早い(早く)
earn **kasegimas'** (*kasegu, kaseide*) かせぐ
earnest **majime (na)** まじめ(な)
earth **tsuchi** 土
earthenware **doki** 土器
earthquake **jishin** 地震
east **higashi** 東
easy **yasashii** やさしい
eat **tabemas'** (*taberu, tabete*) 食べる
echo **hibiki** 響き
economics **keizai** 経済 「検約する
economize **ken-yaku shimas'** (*suru, sh'te*)
edge **fuchi** ふち; (*of knife*) **ha** 刃
education **kyōiku** 教育
eel **unagi** うなぎ 「**kiki-me** 利目
effect (*result*) **kekka** 結果; (*effectiveness*)
(is) effective **kikimas'** (*kiku, kiite*) 利く
efficiency **nōritsu** 能率
effort **hone-ori** 骨折り
egg **tamago** 卵
eight **hachi** 八 *or* **yattsu** 八つ
eighteen **jū hachi** 十八
eighty **hachi-jū** 八十
either one **dochira de mo** どちらでも
elastic (*material*) **gomu** ゴム
elbow **hiji** 肘
elect **erabimas'** (*erabu, erande*) 選ぶ
election **senkyo** 選挙
electricity **denki** 電気

elegant **fūryū (na)** 風流(な)
elephant **zō** 象
elevator **erebētā** エレベーター
eleven **jū ichi** 十一
else **hoka ni** 外に 「困る
embarrassed **komarimas'** (*komaru, komatte*)
embassy **taishikan** 大使館 「**sama** 天皇様
Emperor **Tennō-heika** 天皇陛下 *or* **Tennō-**
employ **yatoimas'** (*yatou, yatotte*) 雇う
(is) employed **tsutomete imas'** (*iru, ite*)
 勤めている 「皇后様
Empress **Kōgō-heika** 皇后陛下 *or* **Kōgō-sama**
empty **kara (no)** から(の) *or* **karappo (no)**
 からっぽ(の) 「*owatte*) 終る
end **owari** 終り; (*it ends*) **owarimas'** (*owaru,*
(goes to the) end (of a road, etc.) **ts'ki-**
 atarimas' (*-ataru, -atatte*) 突き当る
enema **kanchō** 灌腸
enemy **teki** 敵
energy **ikioi** 勢
engaged (to be married) **kon-yaku sh'te**
 imas' (*iru, ite*) 婚約している
engagement (*date*) **yak'soku** 約束
engine **kikan** 機関
engineer **gishi** 技師
England **Eikoku** 英国
English **Eigo** 英語
Englishman **Eikoku-jin** 英国人 「楽しむ
enjoy **tanoshimimas'** (*tanoshimu, tanoshinde*)

enough **jūbun (na)** 充分(な)
ensign **shōi** 少尉
enter **(... ni** *or* **... no naka ni) hairimas'** (*hairu, haitte*) (の中に) 入る 「馳走する
entertain **gochisō shimas'** (*suru, sh'te*) 御
enthusiastic **nesshin (na)** 熱心(な)
entire **zentai no** 全体の
entrance **iri-guchi** 入口
envelope **fūtō** 封筒 「うらやむ
envy **urayamimas'** (*urayamu, urayande*)
equal **hitoshii** 等しい
equipment **sōchi** 装置 *or* **setsubi** 設備
erase **keshimas'** (*kesu, kesh'te*) 消す
eraser (*pencil*) **keshi-gomu** 消ゴム; (*blackboard*) **kokuban-fuki** 黒板ふき
erect **tatemas'** (*tateru, tatete*) 建てる
erotic **iroppoi** 色っぽい *or* **kōshoku** 好色
errand **ts'kai** 使い
errand boy **o-ts'kai san** お使いさん
error **machigai** 間違い
escape **nigemas'** (*nigeru, nigete*) 逃げる
especially **tokubetsu ni** 特別に *or* **koto ni**
essential **hitsuyō (na)** 必要(な) し殊に
establish **tatemas'** (*tateru, tatete*) 建てる
etiquette **reigi** 礼儀
Europe **Yōroppa** ヨーロッパ
evaporated milk **nōshuku gyūnyū** 濃縮牛乳 *or* **kona-miruku** 粉ミルク
even ... **... de mo**

evening **ban** 晩 *or* **yūgata** 夕方
ever (*once*) **itsu ka** いつか; (*always*) **itsu mo** いつも
every . . . **dono . . . de mo** どのでも
everybody **minna** 皆 *or* **dare de mo** 誰でも
everything **minna** 皆 *or* **nan de mo** 何でも
everywhere **doko ni mo** どこにも *or* **doko de mo** どこでも
evil *see* bad
exact (*detailed*) **kuwashii** 詳しい; (*correct*) **seikaku (na)** 正確(な)
exactly **chōdo** 丁度 *or* **mattaku** 全く
examination **sh'ken** 試験
example **rei** 例
excellent **sugureta** すぐれた
except (for) . . . **. . . no hoka** の外
exception **reigai** 例外
excessive **yokei (na)** 余計(な)
exchange **tori-kaemas'** (*-kaeru, -kaete*) 取換える *or* **kōkan shimas'** (*suru, sh'te*) 交換する
(gets) excited **ki ga tachimas'** (*tatsu, tatte*) 気が立つ
excursion **ensoku** 遠足 *or* **yūran** 遊覧
Excuse me. **Sumimasen.** すみません *or* **Gomen nasai.** ごめんなさい
exercise (*physical*) **taisō** 体操
existence **sonzai** 存在
exit **deguchi** 出口
expect (*await*) **matte imas'** (*iru, ite*) 待っている
expects to (do) **. . . (suru) tsumori des'** (する) つもりです

expensive (**ne ga**) **takai** (値が)高い
experience **keiken** 経験
expert **jōzu** (**na**) 上手 (な) *or* **tassha** (**na**) 「達者(な)
explain **setsumei shimas'** (*suru, sh'te*) 説明する
export **yushutsu shimas'** (*suru, sh'te*) 輸出する
extend **nobashimas'** (*nobasu, nobash'te*) 伸ばす
extra **yobun ni** 余分に *or* **betsu** (**na**) 別 (な)
extravagance **zeitaku** 贅沢
extremely **hijō ni** 非常に *or* **kiwamete** 極めて
or **hanahada** はなはだ *or* **shigoku** 至極
⌊*or* **mono-sugoku** ものすごく
eye **me** 目
eyebrow **mayuge** まゆげ

F

fabric **orimono** 織物
face **kao** 顔
fact **jijitsu** 事実 *or* **koto** 事: (*in . . .*) **jitsu** 「**wa** 実は
factory **kōba** 工場
fade **samemas'** (*sameru, samete*) 褪める
fail (*in school, etc.*) **rakudai shimas'** (*suru, sh'te*) 落第する
faint **ki o ushinaimas'** (*ushinau, ushinatte*) 「気を失う
fair (*just*) **kōhei** (**na**) 公平(な)
fair (*market*) **ichi** 市
fake **nisemono** にせもの
fall **ochimas'** (*ochiru, och'te*) 落ちる *or* **okkochimas'** (*okkochiru, okkoch'te*)
false **uso** 嘘

false teeth **ire-ba** 入歯
familiar **shitashii** 親しい
family **uchi** 家 *or* **kazoku** 家族
famous **yūmei na** 有名な *or* **na-dakai** 名高い
fan (*folding*) **sensu** 扇子; (*flat*) **uchiwa** うちわ
far **tōi** 遠い ⌊(*electric*) **sempūki** 扇風機
farmer **hyak'shō** 百姓
fast **hayaku, hayai** 速く(い)
fat (*gets fat*) **f'torimas'** (*f'toru, f'totte*) 肥る,
(*is fat*) **f'totte imas'** (*iru, ite*) 肥っています
fate **un** 運
father **otōsan** お父さん *or* **chichi(-oya)** 父(親)
Father . . . (*Reverend*) . . . **Shimpu san** 神
父さん ⌈**desh'ta.** (私が)悪いでした
(It was my) fault. (**Watashi ga**) **warui**
favor **shinsetsu** 親切
favorite **ichiban s'ki** (**na**) 一番好き(な)
fear **osoremas'** (*osoreru, osorete*) 恐れる
feather **hane** 羽
February **Ni-gatsu** 二月
feeble **yowai** 弱い ⌈食べさせる
feed **tabesasemas'** (*tabesaseru, tabesasete*)
feel (*by touch*) **sawarimas'** (*sawaru, sawatte*)
触る; (*by emotion*) **kanjimas'** (*kanjiru,*
feeling **kimochi** 気持 ⌊*kanjite*) 感じる
(it) feels (good) **kimochi ga ii** 気持がいい
fellow **hito** 人 *or* **mono** 者
female **onna** 女
fence **kakine** 垣根

ferryboat **watashi-bune** 渡し舟
festival **matsuri** 祭
feudal (system) **hōken(-seido)** 封建制度
fever **netsu** 熱
few **s'koshi (no)** 少し(の); **s'kunai** 少い
fickle **uwaki (na)** 浮気(な) 「田圃
field (*dry*) **hatake** 畑; (*rice*) **ta** 田 *or* **tambo**
fierce **hageshii** 烈しい *or* **sugoi** すごい
fifteen **jū go** 十五
fifty **go-jū** 五十
fight **tatakaimas'** (*tatakau, tatakatte*) 戦う
figure *see* count; *see* think; *see* body
file (*like nail file*) **yasuri** やすり
fill **ippai ni shimas'** (*suru, sh'te*) 一杯にする
film **fuirumu** フィルム
filthy *see* dirty
finance **zaisei** 財政 「ける
find **mits'kemas'** (*mits'keru, mits'kete*) 見付
fine *see* good
finger **yubi** 指
finish *see* end; (*finishes it*) **sumashimas'** (*sumasu, sumash'te*) すます
fire **hi** 火; (*accidental*) **kaji** 火事
fire (*dismiss, discharge*) (**. . . ni**) **hima o dashimas'** (*dasu, dash'te*) 暇を出す
fire hydrant **shōbōsen** 消防栓
fireman **shōbōfu** 消防夫
fireworks **hana-bi** 花火
first **hajime no** 初めの *or* **saisho no** 最初の;

(*class in trains, etc.*) **ittō** 一等; (*of hotels, etc.*) **ichi-ryū** (**no**) 一流(の)
fish **sakana** 魚
fisherman **gyofu** 漁夫
fishing (*as sport*) **tsuri** 釣
fist **kobushi** こぶし
five **go** 五 *or* **itsutsu** 五つ
fix (*repair*) **naoshimas'** (*naosu, naosh'te*) 直す
flag **hata** 旗
flashlight **kaichū-dentō** 懐中電灯
flat **taira** (**na**) 平(な)
flatulence **onara** おなら
flea **nomi** のみ
flesh **nikutai** 肉体
float **ukabimas'** (*ukabu, ukande*) 浮ぶ
flood **ōmizu** 大水
floor **yuka** 床
florist **hana-ya** 花屋
flour **ko** 粉; (*wheat*) **meriken-ko** メリケン粉
flow **nagaremas'** (*nagareru, nagarete*) 流れる
flower **hana** 花
flower arrangement **o-hana** お花 *or* (arranging) **ikebana** 生花
flowerpot **ueki-bachi** 植木鉢
flower viewing **hana-mi** 花見
fly (*insect*) **hae** はえ
fly (*moves in air*) **tobimas'** (*tobu, tonde*) 飛ぶ
foam *see* bubble
focus **pinto** ピント
fog **kiri** 霧
fold up **ori-tatamimas'** (*-tatamu, -tatande*) 折りたたむ

folks *see* people; *see* parents; *see* family
follow **. . . no ato o ts'kemas'** (*ts'keru, ts'kete*) の後を附ける
following **tsugi** (**no**) 次(の)
fond of *see* like
food **tabemono** 食べ物 *or* **gohan** 御飯; (American) **yōshoku** 洋食; (Japanese) **washoku** 和食
fool **baka** ばか
foolish **baka-rashii** ばからしい *or* **baka** (**na**) ばか(な)
foot **ashi** 足
footstool **ashi-dai** 足台
for (**no**) **tame** (**ni**) (の)ため(に)
forbid **kinjimas'** (*kinjiru, kinjite*) 禁じる
force (to do) **muri ni** (*or* **shiite**) **sasemas'** (*saseru, sasete*) 無理に(強いて)させる
foreign **gaikoku** (**no**) 外国(の)
foreigner **gaijin** 外人
forest **hayashi** 林 *or* **mori** 森
forever *see* always
forget **wasuremas'** (*wasureru, wasurete*) 忘れる
forgive **yurushimas'** (*yurusu, yurush'te*) 許す
fork **fōku** フォーク *or* **hōku** ホーク
form **katachi** 形
former **mae no** 前の
fortune **zaisan** 財産; (*luck*) **un** 運
fortunetelling **uranai** 占い
forty **yon-jū** *or* **shi-jū** 四十
forward **mae ni** 前に
foul *see* dirty
found *see* find; *see* establish

fountain pen **mannenhitsu** 万年筆
four **yon** *or* **shi** 四 *or* **yottsu** 四つ
four people **yo-nin** 四人
four o'clock **yo-ji** 四時
fourteen **jū yon** *or* **jū shi** 十四
fox **kitsune** 狐
fragile **koware-yasui** こわれやすい
frame **waku** 枠
France **Furansu** フランス
free (*gratis*) **tada** (**no**) 只の; (*as part of the service*) **sābisu** サービス
freely **jiyū ni** 自由に
freeze (*it freezes*) **kōrimas'** (*kōru, kōtte*) 凍る; (*freezes it*) **kōrasemas'** (*kōraseru, kōrasete*) 凍らせる
French (language) **Furansu-go** フランス語
frequently *see* often
fresh **atarashii** 新らしい
Friday **kin-yōbi** 金曜日
friend **tomodachi** 友達
frog **kaeru** 蛙
from . . . **. . . kara** から
front **mae** 前
frost **shimo** 霜
fruit **kudamono** 果物
fry **agemas'** (*ageru, agete*) 揚げる
frying pan **age-nabe** あげなべ
Fuji-yama **Fuji(-san)** 富士(山)
full **ippai** (**no**) 一杯(の)

fun **omoshiroi koto** おもしろい事
(This is) fun! **Omoshiroi des' ne!** おもしろいですね
funeral **o-sōsh'ki** お葬式
funnel **rōto** 漏斗
funny **okashii** おかしい *or* **kokkei (na)** こっけい(な) *or* **yukai (na)** 愉快(な)
fur **ke-gawa** 毛皮
furnace **kamado** かまど
furnish (*provide*) **sonaemas'** (*sonaeru, sonaete*) 備える
furniture **kagu** 家具
further **hoka (ni)** 外(に)
fuss **sawagi** 騒ぎ
futile **muda** むだ
future **shōrai** 将來

G

gain *see* get
gambling **tobaku** とばく *or* **bakuchi** ばくち
game **asobi** 遊び *or* **gēmu** ゲーム
gap **s'kima** 隙間
garbage **gomi** ごみ
garbage man **gomi-ya** ごみ屋
garden **niwa** 庭
gardener **ueki-ya** 植木屋
garlic **ninniku** にんにく
garter **gātā** ガーター
gas **gasu** ガス; (*gasoline*) **gasorin** ガソリン

gas(oline) station **gasorin s'tando** ガソリン・スタンド
gasp **aegimas'** (*aegu, aeide*) 喘ぐ
gate **mon** 門
gather (*they gather*) **atsumarimas'** (*atsumaru, atsumatte*) 集まる; (*gathers them*) **atsumemas'** (*atsumeru, atsumete*) 集める
gaudy **hade (na)** はで(な)
gay **akarui** 明るい *or* **yukai (na)** 愉快(な)
general (*over-all*) **ippan (no)** 一般(の)
general (*army*) **taishō** 大将
generous **kandai (na)** 寛大な
gentle **yasashii** やさしい
gentleman **shinshi** 紳士
genuine **hommono (no)** 本物(の) *or* **makoto (no)** 真(の)
geography **chiri** 地理
geology **chishitsu** 地質
germ **baikin** ばい菌
German (language) **Doitsu-go** ドイツ語
Germany **Doitsu** ドイツ
gesture **temane** 手まね
get (*receive*) **moraimas'** (*morau, moratte*) 貰う; *see also* go, buy, take, become, etc.
get off (*get down*) **orimas'** (*oriru, orite*) 下りる
get up (*arise*) **okimas'** (*okiru, okite*) 起きる
ghost **obake** お化け *or* **bakemono** 化物
gift **okurimono** 贈り物
ginger **shōga** しょうが
girdle **koshi-obi** 腰帯

girl **musume (san)** むすめ(さん)
gist **yōshi** 要旨 *or* **yōten** 要点
give 1. (*he to you, you to me*) **kuremas'** (*kureru, kurete*) 呉れる *or* **kudasaimas'** (*kudasaru, kudasatte*) 下さる 2. (*I to you, you to him, he to him*) **agemas'** (*ageru, agete*) 上げる *or* **yarimas'** (*yaru, yatte*) やる
gladly **yorokonde** 喜んで
glass (*the substance*) **garasu** ガラス; (*the container*) **koppu** コップ, **gurasu** グラス, **gurasu-koppu** グラス・コップ
glasses **megane** めがね
gloomy **uttōshii** うっとうしい
glove **tebukuro** 手袋
glow **hikarimas'** (*hikaru, hikatte*) 光る
glue **nikawa** にかわ
glutinous rice **mochi-gome** もち米
go **ikimas'** (*iku, itte*) 行く
goat **yagi** やぎ
God **Kami(-sama)** 神(様)
godown (*storeroom*) **kura** 倉
gold **kin** 金
gonorrhea **rimbyō** 痳病
good **ii** いい *or* **yoi** よい
Good-bye. **Sayōnara** さようなら
goods **shinamono** 品物
goose **gachō** がちょう
gorgeous **rippa (na)** 立派(な)
gossip **uwasa** うわさ

government **seifu** 政府

governor **chiji** 知事 「少しずつ

gradually **dandan** だんだん *or* **s'koshi zutsu**

graduate **sotsugyō shimas'** (*suru, sh'te*)
卒業する 「穀物

grain (*one*) **tsubu** つぶ; (*cereal*) **kokumotsu**

grammar **bumpō** 文法

grand **subarashii** 素晴しい *or* **erai** えらい

grandchild **mago** 孫

grandfather **ojii-san** おじいさん

grandmother **obaa-san** おばあさん

grapes **budō** ぶどう

grass **k'sa** 草

(I am) grateful. **Arigataku zonjimas'.** (*zonjiru, zonjite*) ありがたく存じます

grave (*tomb*) **haka** 墓 「(**no**) ねずみ色(の)

gray **hai-iro (no)** 灰色(の) *or* **nezumi-iro**

grease **abura** あぶら

great *see* big; *see* good

greedy **kui-shimbō (na)** 食いしん坊(な)

green **midori (no)** 緑(の)

greens **aomono** 青物

greeting **aisatsu** 挨拶

grill **aburimas'** (*aburu, abutte*) あぶる

groan **umekimas'** (*umeku, umeite*) うめく

grocery store **shokuryōhin-ten** 食料品店

ground **jimen** 地面

group (*class*) **kumi** 組; (*crowd, flock*) **mure** 群

grow **ōkiku narimas'** (*naru, natte*) 大きくなる

gruel (*rice*) **o-kayu** おかゆ
guard **mamorimas'** (*mamoru, mamotte*) 守る
guess **atemas'** (*ateru, atete*) 当てる; *see also* understand
guest **kyaku** 客, **o-kyaku san** お客さん
guide (*person*) **annai-sha** 案内者; (book) **annai-sho** 案内書; (*guides him*) **annai shimas'** (*suru, sh'te*) 案内する
guilt **tsumi** 罪
gulf **wan** 湾
gull **kamome** かもめ
gum (*chewing*) **gamu** ガム
gun **jū** 銃 *or* **teppō** 鉄砲
gutter **dobu** どぶ

H

habit **shūkan** 習慣; (*bad one*) **kuse** 癖
hail **arare** (**ga furimas;** *furu, futte*) あられ(が降る)
hair (*on head*) **kami** 髪; (*elsewhere*) **ke** 毛
hairdresser *see* beauty parlor
hair oil **kami-abura** 髪油; (*stick pomade*) **chikku** チック
half **hambun** 半分
hall **kaikan** 会館; (*entrance*) **genkan** 玄関
halt *see* stop
ham **hamu** ハム
hammer **kanazuchi** かなづち

hand **te** 手
hand (something to a person) **watashimas'** (*watasu, watash'te*) 渡す
handkerchief **hankechi** ハンケチ
handle **totte** とって(把手)
handy *see* convenient
hangs (*it hangs*) **kakarimas'** (*kakaru, kakatte*) 掛る; (*hangs it*) **kakemas'** (*kakeru, kakete*) 掛ける
happen **okorimas'** (*okoru, okotte*) 起る
happiness **kōf'ku** 幸福
happy **ureshii** うれしい
hard **katai** 堅い
hardly **hotondo** + NEGATIVE (**nai**) ほとんど(ない)
hardware **kanagu** 金具
harm **gai** 害
harp (*Japanese*) **koto** 琴
hash **hayashi** 林
hasten *see* hurry
hat **bōshi** 帽子
hatchet **nata** 鉈 *or* **te-omo** 手斧
hate **iya des'** いやです; **kirai des'** きらいです
have (**. . . ga**) **arimas'** (*aru, atte*) ある *or* **motte imas'** (*iru, ite*) 持っている
hawk **taka** たか
hay **magusa** まぐさ
he **kare** 彼 *or* **ano hito** あの人
head **atama** 頭
headquarters **hombu** 本部 *or* **shireibu** 司令部
health **kenkō** 健康

healthy **genki** (**na**) 元気(な) **jōbu** (**na**) 丈夫(な)
hear **kikimas'** (*kiku, kiite*) 聞く 「**kokoro** 心
heart **shinzō** 心臓; (*as seat of emotions*)
heat **atsu-sa** 暑(熱)さ; (*heats it*) **ats'ku shimas'** (*suru, sh'te*) 熱くする; (*it heats up*) **ats'ku narimas'** (*naru, natte*) 熱くなる
heater **hiitā** ヒーター *or* **kanetsu-ki** 加熱器
heating (*of room, etc.*) **dambō** 暖房
heaven **tengoku** 天国
heavy **omoi** 重い
hedge **ikegaki** 生垣
heel **kakato** かかと
hell **jigoku** 地獄
Hello. (*on phone*) **Moshi moshi.** (*on street, in morning*) **Ohayō gozaimas'.** (*daytime*) **Konnichi wa.** (*evening*) **Komban wa.**
help (*assist*) **tetsudaimas'** (*tetsudau, tetsudatte*) 手伝う; (*save*) **tas'kemas'** (*tas'keru, tas'kete*)
hemorrhoids **ji** 痔 └助ける
her *see* she
here **koko** ここ 「ちょする
hesitate **chūcho shimas'** (*suru, sh'te*) ちゅう
hey! **oi!** おい! *or* **moshi-moshi!** もしもし!
hi! *see* hello; *see* hey
hiccup **shakkuri** しゃっくり
hide (*hides it*) **kakushimas'** (*kakusu, kaku-sh'te*) 隠す; (*it hides*) **kakuremas'** (*kaku-*
high **takai** 高い └*reru, kakurete*) 隠れる
highway **kokudō** 国道 *or* **kōdō** 公道

hill (*road*) **saka** 坂; (*small mountain*) **oka** 丘
him *see* he
hip **koshi** 腰 *or* **shiri** 尻
hire **yatoimas'** (*yatou, yatotte*) 雇う
history **rekishi** 歴史
hit **buts'kemas'** (*buts'keru, buts'kete*) ぶつける
or **uchimas'** (*utsu, utte*) 打つ
hold (**te ni**) **mochimas'** (*motsu, motte*) (手に)持つ
hole **ana** 穴
holiday **yasumi** 休み; (*official*) **saijitsu** 祭日
home **uchi** 家
homesick (**uchi ga**) **natsukashii** (家が)なつかしい
honest **shōjiki** (**na**) 正直(な)
honey **mitsu** 蜜 *or* **hachi-mitsu** はち蜜
honorific (word) **keigo** 敬語
hook **kagi** 鉤
hope **nozomimas'** (*nozomu, nozonde*) 望む
horn (*of animal*) **tsuno** 角
horrible **osoroshii** おそろしい
horse **uma** 馬
horseradish **wasabi** わさび
hospital **byōin** 病院
hot **atsui** 暑(熱)い
hot water **o-yu** お湯
hot-water bottle **yu-tampo** 湯たんぽ
hotel **hoteru** ホテル
hour **jikan** 時間
house **uchi** 家
housewife **shufu** 主婦

how **dō** どう 「しかし
however **keredomo** けれども *or* **sh'kashi**
human being **ningen** 人間 「けんそんする
humble (*modest*) **kenson shimas'** (*suru, sh'te*)
humid (*in summer*) **mushi-atsui** 蒸し暑い;
(*in winter*) **shimeppoi** 湿っぽい
hundred **hyaku** 百 「ました
hungry **onaka ga s'kimash'ta** お腹が空き
hunt **kari** *or* **ryō o shimas'** (*suru, sh'te*)
hurray! **banzai!** 万歳 L狩をする
hurricane **bōfū** 暴風
hurry **isogimas'** (*isogu, isoide*) 急ぐ
hurt **itai des'** 痛いです
husband **danna-san** だんなさん *or* **shujin** 主人
hygiene **eisei** 衛生

I

I **watashi** 私
ice **kōri** 氷
ice cream **ais'-kuriimu** アイスクリーム
idea **kangae** 考
if **moshi** もし
ill *see* sick; *see* bad
illegal **fuhō (na)** 不法(な)
imagine *see* think 「の真似をする
imitate **. . . no mane o shimas'** (*suru, sh'te*)
imitation (*man-made*) **. . . jinzō . . .** 人造
immediately **sugu** すぐ

impatient **ki ga mijikai** 気が短い
Imperial . . . **Teikoku . . .** 帝国
impolite **burei (na)** 無礼(な)
import **yunyū shimas'** (*suru, sh'te*) 輸入する
important **jūyō (na)** 重要 (な) *or* **taisetsu (na)** 大切(な)
impossible **dekinai** 出来ない *or* **fukanō (na)** 「不可能(な)
impression **inshō** 印象
improve (*it improves*) **naorimas'** (*naoru, naotte*) 直る *or* **yoku narimas'** (*naru, natte*) よくなる; (*improves it*) **naoshimas'** (*naosu, naosh'te*) 直す *or* **yoku shimas'** (*suru, sh'te*) よくする
in **. . . ni** に *or* **. . . no naka ni** の中に
incense **kō** 香
inch (*Japanese*) **sun** 寸; (*American*) **inchi** 「インチ
income **shotoku** 所得 *or* **shūnyū** 収入
income tax **shotoku-zei** 所得税
inconvenient **fuben (na)** 不便(な)
increase **mashimas'** (*masu, mash'te*) 増す
indecent **waisetsu (na)** わいせつ(な)
indeed **honto ni** ほんとに
independence **dokuritsu** 独立
India **Indo** インド
indigestion **fushōka** 不消化
indirect **kansetsu (na)** 間接(な)
individually **betsu-betsu ni** 別々に
indoors **uchi (no naka) ni** *or* **de** 家(の中)に *or* で

industry **kōgyō** 工業 *or* **sangyō** 産業
influence **eikyō** 影響
inform **shirasemas'** (*shiraseru, shirasete*) 「知らせる
infrequently **tama ni** たまに *or* **mare ni** 稀に
injection **chūsha** 注射
injury **kega** 怪我
ink **inki** インキ
Inland Sea **Seto-Naikai** 瀬戸内海
inn (*Japanese hotel*) **ryokan** 旅館
inquire *see* ask
insane **ki-chigai** 気違い
insect **mushi** 虫
inside **naka ni** 中に
instead **(sono) kawari ni** (その)代りに
instruct *see* teach
instructor **kyōshi** 教師 *or* **sensei** 先生
insult **bujoku** 侮辱
insurance **hoken** 保険
intelligent **rikō (na)** 利口(な)
intend to (do) **...(suru) tsumori des'** (する)「つもりです
interest (*on mony*) **rishi** 利子
interest (*pleasure*) **kyōmi** 興味
interesting **omoshiroi** おもしろい
interfere **jama ni narimas'** (*naru, natte*) じゃまになる *or* **jama o shimas'** (*suru, sh'te*) じゃまをする
international **kok'sai no** 国際の
interpreter **tsūyaku** 通訳
interview **menkai** 面会

intestines **harawata** 腸
intimate **shitashii** したしい
intoxicated *see* drunk
introduce **shōkai shimas'** (*suru, sh'te*) 紹介する
invention **hatsumei** 発明
investigate **shirabemas'** (*shiraberu, shirabete*) 調べる
invite **yobimas'** (*yobu, yonde*) 呼ぶ *or* **manekimas'** (*maneku, maneite*) 招く *or* **shōtai shimas'** (*suru, sh'te*) 招待する
iodine **yōdo** ヨウド
Ireland **Airurando** アイルランド
iron (*the metal*) **tetsu** 鉄; (*clothes iron*) **airon** アイロン; (*irons clothes*) **kimono ni airon o kakemas'** (*kakeru, kakete*) 着物にアイロンをかける
irregular **fukisoku (na)** 不規則(な)
is (am, are, be) 1. (*it is*) **... des'** (**da** *or* **na** *or* **no, de**) だ 2. (*there is; it is in a place*) **arimas'** (*aru, atte*) ある 3. (*he is in a place*) **imas'** (*iru, ite*) 居る *or* **orimas'** (*oru, otte*) 居る 4. (*is doing*) **...-te imas'** (*iru, ite*) *or* **...-te orimas'** (*oru, otte*) ...て居る
island **shima** 島
isn't (aren't) 1. (*it isn't*) **...ja arimasen** (*ja nai, ja nakute*) じゃない 2. (*there isn't*) **arimasen** (*nai, nakute*) 無い
it *usually omitted in Japanese; or* **sore** それ
Italy **Itariya** イタリヤ
itch(y) **kaii** (*or* **kayui**) かゆい

ivory **zōge** 象牙

J

jade **kōgyoku** 硬玉
jail **rōgoku** 牢獄
jam (*to eat*) **jamu** ジャム
janitor **kozukai** 小使
January **Ichi-gatsu** 一月 *or* **Shōgatsu** 正月
Japan **Nihon** *or* **Nippon** 日本
Japanese (language) **Nihon-go** 日本語
Japanese (*person*) **Nihon-jin** 日本人
Japanese (*of Japan*) **Nihon no** 日本の
jar (*with large mouth*) **kame** かめ; (*with small mouth*) **tsubo** 壷
jaundice **ōdan** 黄疸
jaw **ago** あご
jealous **yakimochi o yakimas'** (*yaku, yaite*) 焼餅を焼く
jelly **zeri** ゼリ *or* **jeri** ジェリ
jellyfish **kurage** くらげ
Jew **Yudaya-jin** ユダヤ人
jewel **hōseki** 宝石
job **shigoto** 仕事
join (*joins them together*) **awasemas'** (*awaseru, awasete*) 合せる; (*enters*) **... ni hairimas'** (*hairu, haitte*) に入る
joke **jōdan** じょうだん(冗談)
journey *see* trip
judge **saiban-kan** 裁判官
juice **jūsu** ジュース; **shiru** 汁

July **Shichi-gatsu** 七月
jump **tobimas'** (*tobu, tonde*) 跳ぶ
June **Roku-gatsu** 六月
just (*exact*) **chōdo** ちょうど(丁度)

K

keep **tamochimas'** (*tamotsu, tamotte*) 保つ
ketchup **kechappu** ケチャップ
kettle **kama** 釜
key **kagi** 鍵
kick **kerimas'** (*keru, kette*) 蹴る
kidneys **jinzō** 腎臓
kill **koroshimas'** (*korosu, korosh'te*) 殺す
kind (*nice*) **shinsetsu (na)** 親切(な)
kind (*variety*) **shurui** 種類
kindergarten **yōchien** 幼稚園
king **ō-sama** 王様 ⌈*suru, sh'te*) **(する)**
kiss **kisu** キス *or* **seppun** 接吻 **(shimas';**
kitchen **daidokoro** 台所
kite **tako** たこ
knee **hiza** 膝
knife **naifu** ナイフ; (*big*) **hōchō** 庖丁
knit **amimas'** (*amu, ande*) 編む
knitted goods **meriyasu** メリヤス
knock (on door) **(to o) tatakimas'** (*tataku,*
tataite) (戸を) たたく
knot **musubi(-me)** 結び(目)
know **shitte imas'** (*iru, ite*) 知っている

Korea **Chōsen** 朝鮮 *or* **Kankoku** 韓国
Korean (language) **Chōsen-go** 朝鮮語
Korean (*person*) **Chōsen-jin** 朝鮮人
Kurile Islands **Chishima Rettō** 千島列島

L

labor *see* work
lace *see* shoelace
lacquer **urushi** 漆; (*lacquer ware*) **nurimono** 塗物; (*raised lacquer*) **maki-e** 蒔絵
ladder **hashigo** はしご
lady **fujin** 婦人
lake **mizuumi** 湖
lamb (*meat*) **yōniku** 羊肉
lame **chimba** ちんば
lamp **rampu** ランプ
land *see* country; *see* earth; *see* place; (*come ashore*) **jōriku shimas'** (*suru, sh'te*) 上陸する; (*from the air*) **chakuriku shimas'** (*suru, sh'te*) 着陸する
landlord **shujin** 主人
language **kotoba** ことば *or* **gengo** 言語
lantern (*of paper*) **chōchin** 提灯
lap **hiza** 膝
large *see* big; *see* wide
large-size (model) **ōgata** 大型
last (*final*) **owari no** 終りの *or* **saigo no** 最後の; (*preceding*) **kono mae no** この前の

last night **kinō no ban** (*or* **sakuban**) 昨(日の)晩 *or* **yūbe** ゆうべ 「*rete*) 遅れる
late **osoi** 遅い *or* **okuremas'** (*okureru, oku-*
latrine *see* toilet
laugh **waraimas'** (*warau, waratte*) 笑う
laundry **sentaku** 洗濯
lavatory *see* bathroom; *see* toilet
lawn **shibafu** 芝生
lawn mower **shiba-kari** 芝刈
lawyer **bengoshi** 弁護士
lay (*put*) **okimas'** (*oku, oite*) 置く; (*lie down*) **nemas'** (*neru, nete*) 寝る
lazy (*person*) **namake-mono** なまけもの
lead (*metal*) **namari** 鉛 「案内する
lead (*guide*) **annai shimas'** (*suru, sh'te*)
leaf **happa** 葉っぱ
leak **morimas'** (*moru, motte*) 漏る
learn **naraimas'** (*narau, naratte*) 習う
leave **demas'** (*deru, dete*) 出る; (*for a long distance*) **tachimas'** (*tatsu, tatte*) 立つ
lecture **kōgi** 講義
left **hidari** (**no**) 左(の)
leg **ashi** 足 「伝説
legend **mukashi-banashi** 昔話 *or* **densetsu**
leisure **hima** ひま
lemon **remon** レモン
lend **kashimas'** (*kasu, kash'te*) 貸す
lens **renzu** レンズ
less (**yori**) **s'kunai** (より)少ない

lesson **ka** 課; (*takes lessons*) **naraimas'** (*narau, naratte*) 習う

let **sasemas'** (*saseru, sasete*) させる *or* **yurushimas'** (*yurusu, yurush'te*) 許す

let out (of vehicle) **oroshimas'** (orosu, orosh'te) 下ろす

letter **tegami** 手紙; (*of the alphabet, etc.*) **moji** 文字

lever **teko** てこ

lewd **s'kebē (na)** すけべえ(な)

library (*building*) **toshokan** 図書館; (*room*) **tosho-shitsu** 図書室

lice **shirami** しらみ

license **menkyo** 免許

lick **namemas'** (*nameru, namete*) 嘗める

lid **f'ta** ふた(蓋)

lie (*falsehood*) **uso** うそ

lie (down) **nemas'** (*neru, nete*) 寝る

lieutenant (*1st Lt, Lt JG*) **chū-i** 中尉; (*2nd Lt*) **shō-i** 少尉; (*full navy*) **tai-i** 大尉

life **inochi** 命

lift **agemas'** (*ageru, agete*) 上げる

light (*electric*) **denki** 電気 *or* **dentō** 電燈; (*bright*) **akarui** 明るい

light (*weight*) **karui** 軽い

lighter (*cigarette*) **raitā** ライター

lightning **inabikari** いな光 *or* **inazuma** いなづま

like (*fond of*) **s'ki des'** 好きです *or* **s'kimas'** (*s'ku, suite*) 好く

like (*similar to*) **...ni nite imas'** (*iru, ite*) に似ている

lily **yuri** ゆり

limit **kagiri** 限り

line **sen** 線

linen **ama** あま(亜麻), **rinneru** リンネル

linguistics (*language learning*) **gogaku** 語学; (*science of language*) **gengo-gaku** 言語学

lining **ura** 裏

lion **raion** ライオン *or* **shishi** しし

lip **kuchibiru** 唇

liquid **mizu** 水 *or* **ekitai** 液体

liquor **o-sake** お酒

list (*of items*) **hyō** 表; (*puts in a list*) **hyō ni shimas'** (*suru, sh'te*) 表にする

listen **kikimas'** (*kiku, kiite*) 聞く

literature **bungaku** 文学

little **chiisai** 小さい *or* **chitchai** 小っちゃい

live (*inhabits*) **sunde imas'** (*iru, ite*) 住んでいる; (*exists*) **ikite imas'** (*iru,ite*) 生きている

liver **kimo** 肝 *or* **kanzō** 肝臓; (*as food*) **rebā** レバー

loan *see* lend

lobster **ise-ebi** いせえび

local **chihō no** 地方の; (*of the city*) **machi no** 町の

lock **jō** 錠; (*locks a door*) (**to ni**) **kagi o kakemas'** (*kakeru, kakete*) (戸に)かぎをかける

log **maruta** 丸太

loincloth **fundoshi** ふんどし

lonely **hitori-botchi** 一人ぼっち *or* **sabishii** さびしい

long **nagai** 長い

look **mimas'** (*miru, mite*) 見る

lose **nakushimas'** (*nakusu, nakush'te*) 無くす

or **ushinaimas'** (*ushinau, ushinatte*) 失う
(gets) lost **(michi ni) mayoimas'** (*mayou, mayotte*) (道に) 迷う
lots **tak'san** 沢山
lotus **hasu** 蓮
loud (*noise*) **ōkii** 大きい; (*color*) **hade (na)** はで(な)
loud-speaker **kakusei-ki** 拡声器
louse *see* lice
love **ai shimas'** (*suru, sh'te*) 愛する; *see also* like
lover **koibito** 恋人 *or* **ii-hito** いい人
low **hikui** 低い
luck **un** 運
lucky **un ga ii** 運がいい
luggage **te-nimotsu** 手荷物
lumber **zaimoku** 材木
lump **katamari** 塊
lunch **hiru-gohan** 昼御飯
lungs **hai** 肺
luxury **zeitaku** 贅沢

M

machine **kikai** 機械
mad *see* angry; *see* insane
made in Japan **Nihon-sei (no)** 日本製(の)
magazine **zasshi** 雑誌
maid **jochū** 女中
mail **yūbin** 郵便
main **omo na** 主な *or* **shuyō na** 主要な
major (*army*) **shōsa** 少佐

make (*do*) **shimas'** (*suru, sh'te*) する; (*put together*) **ts'kurimas'** (*ts'kuru, ts'kutte*) 作る *or* **koshiraemas'** (*koshiraeru, koshiraete*) こしらえる
male **otoko** 男
man (*male*) **otoko** 男; (*human*) **hito** 人
manage **tori-atsukaimas'** (*-atsukau, -atsukatte*) 取り扱う
manage (to do) **dō ni ka (shimas'**; *suru, sh'te*) どうにか (する)
Manchuria **Manshū** 満洲
mandarin orange *see* tangerine
manner (of doing) **yarikata** やり方
manners *see* etiquette
manuscript **genkō** 原稿
many **tak'san no** 沢山の *or* **ōku no** 多くの
map **chizu** 地図
maple **momiji** もみじ
March **San-gatsu** 三月
marines **kaiheitai** 海兵隊 *or* **rik'sentai** 陸戦隊
mark **shirushi (o ts'kemas;** *ts'keru, ts'kete*) 印 (を付ける)
market **ichi(-ba)** 市 (場)
marriage **kekkon** 結婚
marry **kekkon shimas'** (*suru, sh'te*) 結婚する
marvellous **sugoi** すごい
mask **men** 面; (*used in Noh drama*) **nō-men** 能面
masturbate **shuin o shimas'** (*suru, sh'te*) 手淫をする *or* (*vulgar*) **senzuri o kakimas'** (*kaku, kaite*) センズリをかく
mat (*Japanese floor*) **tatami** 畳
match (*for fire*) **matchi** マッチ

material *see* cloth
materials **zairyō** 材料 *or* **shiryō** 資料
matter **koto** 事
(It doesn't) matter. **Kamaimasen.**
(What's the) matter? **Dō sh'tan' des' ka?**
May **Go-gatsu** 五月
may (*perhaps*) **...ka mo shiremasen** かも知れません; (*is OK to*) **...-te mo ii des'** ...てもいいです
mayor **shichō** 市長
me **watashi** 私 *or* **watak'shi** 私
meal **gohan** ご飯 *or* **shokuji** 食事
meaning **imi** 意味
measure **hakarimas'** (*hakaru, hakatte*) 計る
meat **niku** 肉
medicine **k'suri** 薬
medium-rare (meat) **han-nie** 半にえ *or* **han-yake** 半焼け
medium-size (model) **chūgata** 中型
meet **...ni aimas'** (*au, atte*) に会う
melon **uri** 瓜
melt (*it melts*) **tokemas'** (*tokeru, tokete*) 溶ける; (*melts it*) **tokashimas'** (*tokasu, tokash'te*) 溶かす
memory **(mono-)oboe** (もの)覚え
mend **naoshimas'** (*naosu, naosh'te*) 直す
menstruation **gekkei** 月経
mental **seishin (no)** 精神(の)
menu **kondate** 献立
merchant **shōnin** 商人
(It's a) mess! **Taihen des' ne.** 大変ですね

message **kotozuke** 言づけ
messy **kitanai** きたない
metal **kane** 金
method **shikata** 仕方 *or* **hōhō** 方法
middle **mannaka** まん中
midnight **ma-yonaka** 真夜中
might *see* perhaps
milk **miruku** ミルク, **gyūnyū** 牛乳
million **hyaku-man** 百万
mind **kokoro** 心 *or* **seishin** 精神
(Never) mind. **Kamaimasen.** かまいません
mine (*my*) **watashi no** 私の
minister (*pastor*) **bok'shi** 牧師
minute **fun** 分 (1 **ip-pun,** 3 **sam-pun,** 4 **yom-pun,** 6 **rop-pun,** 8 **hap-pun**)
mirror **kagami** 鏡
Miss . . . . . **san** さん
miss (*long for*) (**. . . ga**) **natsukashii** なつかしい
missionary **senkyōshi** 宣教師
mistake **machigai** 間違
mix (*mixes it*) **mazemas'** (*mazeru, mazete*) 混ぜる; (*it mixes*) **mazarimas'** (*mazaru, mazatte*) 混ざる; **majirimas'** (*majiru, majitte*) 混じる
modern **gendai no** 現代の
modest *see* humble
(just a) moment **chotto** ちょっと
Monday **getsuyōbi** 月曜日
money (**o-**)**kane** (お)金
monkey **saru** さる

month **ts'ki** 月; (*in counting*) **-kagetsu** 箇月
mood **kibun** 気分
moon **ts'ki** 月 *or* **ots'ki-sama** お月様
mop **moppu** モップ
more **motto** もっと *or* **mō s'koshi** もう少し
morning **asa** 朝
mosquito **ka** か(蚊)
mosquito net **kaya** かや
moss **koke** こけ
most . . . **ichiban . . .** 一番
most of . . . **. . . no daibubun** の大部分
moth **shimi** しみ(衣魚) *or* **mushi** 蛾
moth balls **naf'tarin** ナフタリン *or* **shimi-yoke** しみよけ
mother **okāsan** お母さん *or* **haha** 母
motor **hatsudōki** 発動機
motorcycle **ōtobai** オートバイ
mountain **yama** 山
mouse **hatsuka-nezumi** 二十日ねずみ
mousetrap **nezumi-tori** ねずみとり
mouth **kuchi** 口
move (*it moves*) **ugokimas'** (***ugoku, ugoite***) 動く; (*moves it*) **ugokashimas'** (***ugokasu, ugokash'te***) 動かす
movies **eiga** 映画
movie theater **eiga-kan** 映画館
Mr, Mrs . . . **. . . san** さん
much *see* lots
mud **doro** 泥
murder *see* kill

museum **hakubutsu-kan** 博物館; (*art gallery*) **bijutsu-kan** 美術館

mushroom **kinoko** きのこ (*the most popular kinds are* **mats'take** まつたけ [松茸] *and* **shiitake** しいたけ [椎茸])

music **ongaku** 音楽

must **-nakereba narimasen** なければなりません

mustache **kuchi-hige** ロひげ

mustard **karashi** からし

must not **-te wa ikemasen** てはいけません

mutton *see* lamb

my **watashi no** 私の

myself *see* me

mysterious **fushigi (na)** 不思議(な)

N

nail **kugi** 釘; (*finger, toe*) **tsume** 爪

naked **hadaka (no)** 裸(の)

name **namae** 名前

napkin **napukin** ナプキン

narrow **semai** 狭い

natural, nature **shizen (no)** 自然(の)

naughty **wampaku (na)** わんぱく(な)

navel **heso** へそ

navy **kaigun** 海軍

near **chikai** 近い

nearly **hotondo** ほとんど

necessary **hitsuyō (na)** 必要(な)

neck **kubi** 首
necklace **kubi-kazari** 頸飾り
necktie **nekutai** ネクタイ
need (**. . . ga**) **irimas'** (*iru, itte*) 要る
needle **hari** 針
Negro **Kokujin** 黒人
neighbor(ing) **tonari** 隣
neither . . . nor . . . **. . . mo . . . mo** (+NEGATIVE)
nephew **oi** おい(甥) *or* **oigo san** おいごさん
nerve **shinkei** 神経
nervous *see* worried
nest **su** 巣
net **ami** 網
never **kessh'te** けっして
new **atarashii** 新しい
news **nyūsu** ニュース
newspaper **shimbun** 新聞
(Happy) New Year! **Shinnen omedetō.** 新年「おめでとう
next **tsugi** (**no**) 次(の)
nice *see* good
niece **mei** めい(姪) *or* **meigo san** めいごさん
night **yoru** 夜
nightingale **uguisu** うぐいす
nine **kyū** *or* **ku** 九 *or* **kokonotsu** 九つ
nineteen **jū kyū** *or* **jū ku** 十九
ninety **kyū-jū** *or* **ku-jū** 九十
no **iie** いいえ
nobody **dare mo** + NEGATIVE 誰も
noise **oto** 音; (*boisterous*) **sawagi** 騒ぎ

none (*thing*) **hitotsu mo** + NEGATIVE 一つも; (*person*) **hitori mo** + NEGATIVE 一人も
nonsense **baka na koto** ばかな事
noodles **(o-)soba** (お)そば; (*Japanese style*) **udon** うどん; (*Chinese style*) **rāmen** ラーメン
noodle-shop **soba-ya** そばや; **udon-ya** うどんや
noon **hiru** 昼; (*exact time*) **shōgo** 正午
north **kita** 北
nose **hana** 鼻
not VERB NEGATIVE **(-nai** *or* **-anai)**
note *see* letter
nothing **nani mo** + NEGATIVE 何も
notice **...ni ki ga ts'kimas'** (*ts'ku, tsuite*) に気が付く
novel **shōsetsu** 小説
November **Jūichi-gatsu** 十一月
now **ima** 今; (*just ...*) **tadaima** 只今
nowhere **doko ni mo** + NEGATIVE
(gets) numb **shibiremas'** (*shibireru, shibirete*) しびれる
number **kazu** 数
nun **ama** 尼
nurse **kangofu** 看護婦
nut **kenka** 堅果
nylon **nairon** ナイロン

O

obey (*a person*) **(...no) yū koto o kikimas'** (*kiku, kiite*) 言う事を聞く
object (*thing*) **mono** 物; (*goal*) **mokuteki** 目的

obtain *see* get
occasion **toki** 時; (*circumstance*) **ba(w)ai** 場合
Occident **Seiyō** 西洋
occupation (*job*) **shokugyō** 職業; (*of a country*) **senryō** 占領
occupied (*toilets, etc.*) **shiyō-chū** 使用中; (*telephone*) **hanashi-chū** 話中; (*seat*) **kimas'** 来ます; *see also* busy
occur **okorimas'** (*okoru, okotte*) 起る
ocean **taiyō** 大洋
o'clock **-ji** 時
October **Jū-gatsu** 十月
octopus **tako** たこ
oculist **me-isha** 目医者
odd **hen** (**na**) 変(な)
of . . . **. . . no** の
(turn) off (*lights, radio, etc.*) (**. . . o**) **keshimas'** (*kesu, kesh'te*) 消す
office **jimusho** 事務所
office worker **jimuin** 事務員
(an) official **yakunin** 役人
often **yoku** よく *or* **tabitabi** 度々
oil **abura** 油 *or* (*for machines, etc.*) **sekiyu** 石油; (*lubricating, for cars*) **oiru** オイル
ointment **nuri-gusuri** 塗薬
old (*not new*) **furui** 古い; (*not young*) **toshi-totta** 年取った
older **toshi-ue** (**no**) 年上(の)
olive **oriibu** オリーブ
omelet **omuretsu** オムレツ
omit **otoshimas'** (*otosu, otosh'te*) 落す

on . . . ni に *or* **. . . no ue ni** の上に
(turn) on (*lights, radio, etc.*) **(. . . o) ts'kemas'** (*ts'keru, ts'kete*) 付ける
once **ichi-do** 一度 *or* **ik-kai** 一回 「一人
one **ichi** 一 *or* **hitotsu** 一つ; (*person*) **hitori**
oneself **jibun** 自分
onion **negi** ねぎ
only **tada . . .** 只; **. . . dake** だけ
open (*opens it*) **akemas'** (*akeru, akete*) 開ける; (*it opens*) **akimas'** (*aku, aite*) 開く
operation **shujutsu** 手術
opinion **iken** 意見 *or* **kangae** 考え
opium **ahen** あへん
opportunity **kikai** 機会
opposite (*facing*) **mukō (no)** 向う(の); (*contrary*) **gyaku (no)** 逆(の)
or **ka** か *or* **mata wa** 又は
orange **orenji** オレンジ; *see also* tangerine
order (*clothes, meal etc.*) **chūmon shimas'** (*suru, sh'te*) 注文する; (*a person to do something*) **. . . ni ii-ts'kemas'** (*-ts'keru, -ts'kete*) に言いつける
ordinary **futsū no** 普通の 「**dantai** 団体
organization (*setup*) **sosh'ki** 組織; (*group*)
Orient **Tōyō** 東洋
originally **moto wa** 元は
ornament **kazari** 飾り
orphan **koji** 孤児
orphanage **koji-in** 孤児院

other **hoka no** 外の *or* **betsu no** 別の
otherwise **sa-mo-nakereba** *or* **sō ja nai to**
ought to **...sh'ta hō ga ii deshō** *or* **...suru beki des'**
our(s) **watashi-tachi no** 私達の
out **soto e** 外へ; (*is away from home*) **rusu des'** 留守です
outdoors **soto (de)** 外(で)
outside of (*other than*) **...no hoka** の外
oven **tempi** 天火 *or* **kama** かま
over (*above*) **...no ue ni** の上に
over (*finished*) **(...o) ...-te shimatta** しまった *or* **(...o) ...shichatta** しちゃった
over (do, etc.) **(shi-)sugimas'** (*sugiru, sugite*) (し)すぎる
overshoes **amagutsu** 雨靴 *or* **ōbāshūzu** オーバーシューズ
owing to *see* because
owl **fukuro** ふくろ (梟)
own (*possess*) **motte imas'** (*iru, ite*) 持っている; (*one's*) **jibun no** 自分の
oyster **kaki** かき (牡蠣)

P

Pacific Ocean **Taiheiyō** 太平洋
pack (one's bags) **ni-zukuri o shimas'** (*suru, sh'te*) 荷造をする
package **kozutsumi** 小包
page **pēji** ページ
pain **itami** 痛み
paint **penki (o nurimas'; nuru, nutte)** ペンキ(を塗る)

pair *see* two
palace *(in Tokyo)* **kyūjō** 宮城; *(in Kyoto)* **gosho** 御所
pan **nabe** 鍋
pantry **shokki-shitsu** 食器室
pants **zubon** ズボン; *(underpants)* **zubonsh'-ta** ズボン下
paper **kami** 紙; *(newspaper)* **shimbun** 新聞
paradise **tengoku** 天国
paralysis **mahi** まひ
parcel **kozutsumi** 小包
Pardon me. **Shitsurei.** 失礼 *or* **Sumimasen.** すみません *or* **Gomen kudasai.** 御免下さい
paregoric **geri-dome** 下痢止め
parent **oya** 親
parents **ryōshin** 両親
park **kōen** 公園
parrot **ōmu** おうむ
part **bubun** 部分 *or (one)* **ichi-bu** 一部
particular **tokubetsu no** 特別の
partner **aite** 相手
party **enkai** 宴会 *or* **pātē** パーテー
pass *(hand around—at table)* **mawashimas'** *(mawasu, mawash'te)* 回す; *(hand over)* **watashimas'** *(watasu, watash'te)* 渡す; *(go past)* **. . .o tōrimas'** *(tōru, tōtte)* を通る
passport **ryoken** 旅券 *or* **pas'pōto** パスポート
past **kako** 過去
paste **nori (o ts'kemas';** *ts'keru, ts'kete)* のり(を附ける)
pastry **o-kashi** お菓子
patch **tsugimas'** *(tsugu, tsuide)* 継ぐ

path **komichi** 小路
patience **gaman** 我慢
pawnshop **shichi-ya** 質屋
pay (out) **haraimas'** *or* **shi-haraimas'**
peace **heiwa** 平和 ⌊(*harau, haratte*) (支)払う
peach **momo** 桃
pear **nashi** 梨
pearl **shinju** 真珠
peas **endō(-mame)** えんどう(豆)
peel **(...no) kawa o mukimas'** (*muku,*
Peking **Pekin** ペキン ⌊*muite*) 皮をむく
pen **pen** ペン; (*fountain*) **mannen-hitsu**
pencil **empitsu** 鉛筆 ⌊万年筆
people **hito** 人 *or* **hitobito** 人々
pepper **koshō** 胡椒
percent **pāsento** パーセント 「全く(の)
perfect **kanzen (na)** 完全(な) *or* **mattaku (no)**
perfume **kōsui** 香水 「せん *or* **tabun** 多分
perhaps **...ka mo shiremasen** かもしれま
permanent (wave) **pāma** パーマ
person **hito** 人
perspire *see* sweat
petrol *see* gas(oline)
phone *see* telephone
phonograph **chikuonki** 蓄音器
photograph **shashin** 写真
pick *see* choose
pickpocket **suri** すり
pick up **hiroimas'** (*hirou, hirotte*) 拾う

picnic **ensoku** 遠足
picture **e** 絵
(one) piece **(ik)-ko** (一)個 *or* **(hito)tsu** (一)つ; (*cut off something*) **hito-kire** 一切れ
pig **buta** 豚
pigeon **hato** はと
(one) pile **(hito-)yama** (一)山
piles *see* hemorrhoids
pill **gan-yaku** 丸薬
pillow **makura** 枕
pimp **pombiki** ポン引き
pimple **nikibi** にきび
pin (*for hair*) **pin** ピン; (*for sewing*) **hari** 針
pinch **tsunerimas'** (*tsuneru, tsunette*) 抓る
pine (*tree*) **matsu** 松
pink **momo-iro** 桃色 *or* **pinku** ピンク
pipe **paipu** パイプ
pitiful **kawaisō (na)** かわいそう(な)
place **tokoro** 所
plain (*not gaudy*) **jimi (na)** じみ(な)
plan **keikaku** 計画; (*intention*) **tsumori** つもり
plant **uemas'** (*ueru, uete*) 植える
plate **sara** 皿
platform (*at station*) **hōmu** ホーム
play **asobimas'** (*asobu, asonde*) 遊ぶ
play (*drama*) **shibai** 芝居
pleasant **tanoshii** 楽しい
Please. **Dōzo.** どうぞ *or* **. . . -te kudasai.** 下さい *or* **Onegai shimas'.** お願いします

plenty **tak'san** 沢山
. . . p.m. **gogo . . .** 午後
pocket **poketto** ポケット
Pocketbook *see* purse
point **ten** 点
point at **sashimas'** (*sasu, sash'te*) 指す
poison **doku** 毒
pole (*rod*) **bō** 棒 *or* **sao** 竿
police **keisatsu** 警察
policeman **omawari-san** お巡りさん *or* **junsa** 巡査
polish **migakimas'** (*migaku, migaite*) 磨く
polite **teinei (na)** 丁寧(な)
politics **seiji** 政治
pond **ike** 池
poor (*needy*) **bimbō (na)** 貧乏(な); (*unskilful*) **heta (na)** 下手(な); (*bad*) **warui** 悪い
popular **ninki ga arimas'** (*aru, atte*) 人気がある *or* **hayarimas'** (*hayaru, hayatte*) はやる
population **jinkō** 人口
porcelain **jiki** 磁器
porch **genkan** 玄関
pork **buta-niku** 豚肉
pork cutlet **ton-katsu** 豚カツ
pornography **shunga** 春画
port **minato** 港
porter (*redcap*) **akabō** 赤帽; (*pullman*) **puruman** プルマン
position *see* place; *see* job
possess *see* own
possible **dekimas'** (*dekiru, dekite*) 出来る

post card **hagaki** 葉書; (*picture post card*) **e-hagaki** 絵葉書

post office **yūbin kyoku** 郵便局

pot **hachi** 鉢

potato (*Irish*) **jagaimo** じゃがいも; (*sweet*) **imo** いも *or* **satsuma-imo** さつまいも; (*baked sweet potato*) **yaki-imo** 焼いも

pottery **yakimono** 焼物 *or* **tōki** 陶器

pound (*weight or money*) **pondo** ポンド

pour **tsugimas'** (*tsugu, tsuide*) *or* **sosogimas'** (*sosogu, sosoide*) 注ぐ

powder (*face*) **oshiroi** おしろい

power **chikara** 力

practice (*drill*) **renshū** 練習

pray **inorimas'** (*inoru, inotte*) 祈る 「ん)

preacher (*Protestant*) **bokushi (san)** 牧師(さ

prefer **. . . no hō ga s'ki des'** の方が好きです

pregnancy **ninshin** 妊娠

pregnant **ninshin (shimas'; *suru, sh'te*)** 妊娠

preparation(s) **jumbi** 準備 L(する)

prescription **shohō** 処方

present (*gift*) **okurimono** 贈り物 *or* **purezento** プレゼント; (*as souvenir*) **omiyage** おみやげ

president (*of a nation*) **daitōryō** 大統領

press (on) **oshimas'** (*osu, osh'te*) 押す

pretty **kirei (na)** きれい(な) 「をする

prevent **jama o shimas'** (*suru, sh'te*) じゃま

price **nedan** 値段

priest **shimpu (san)** 神父(さん)
prime minister **shusō** 首相
prison *see* jail
private (use) **shiyō (no)** 私用(の); (*undisturbed*) **jama sarenai** じゃまされない
probably **tabun** 多分 *or* **osoraku** 恐らく *or* **... (suru) deshō** (する) でしょう
problem **mondai** 問題
produce (**... ga**) **dekimas'** (*dekiru, dekite*) 出来る *or* (**... o**) **tsukurimas'** (*tsukuru, tsukutte*) 作る
professor **kyōju** 教授
promise **yak'soku (shimas'**; *suru, sh'te*) 約束(する)
pronunciation **hatsuon** 発音
propaganda **senden** 宣伝
proper **tekitō (na)** 適当(な)
prostitute **jorō** 女郎
protect **mamorimas'** (*mamoru, mamotte*) 守る
proud of (**... o**) **jiman shimas'** (*suru, sh'te*) 自慢する
province (*of Japan*) **ken** 県
public **kōshū (no)** 公衆(の)
pull **hipparimas'** (*hipparu, hippatte*) 引張る *or* **hikimas'** (*hiku, hiite*) 引く
pure **junsui (na)** 純粋(な)
purple **murasaki (no)** 紫(の)
purpose (*intention*) **tsumori** つもり; (*goal*) **mokuteki** 目的; (on) purpose **waza to** わざと
purse **saifu** *or* **gamaguchi** がまぐち
pus **umi** 膿(うみ)
push **oshimas'** (*osu, osh'te*) 押す

put **okimas'** (*oku, oite*) 置く
puzzle **nazo** なぞ

Q

quality **hinshitsu** 品質
quantity **ryō** 量 「(する)
quarrel **kenka** (**shimas'**; *suru, sh'te*) けんか
queen **joō** 女王
queer **hen** (**na**) 変(な) *or* **okashii** おかしい
question **shitsumon** 質問
quick **hayai** 早い; (*quickly*) **hayaku** 早く
quiet **shizuka** (**na**) 静か(な)
quilt **futon** ふとん
quit **yamemas'** (*yameru, yamete*) 止める
quite **sōtō** 相当 *or* **daibu** 大分

R

rabbit **usagi** うさぎ 「**keiba** 競馬
race **kyōsō** 競争; (*cycles*) **keirin** 競輪; (*horse*)
race track **keiba-jō** 競馬場
race (*peoples*) **jinshu** 人種; (*human*) **jinrui** 人類 「(装置)
radiator (*in house, etc.*) **dambō**(**-sōchi**) 煖房
radio **rajio** ラジオ
radish (*Japanese*) **daikon** 大根
raft **ikada** 筏
rag **boro** ぼろ

ragpicker **kuzu-hiroi** くず拾い *or* **bataya** しばたや
railroad **tetsudō** 鉄道
railroad station **eki** 駅
rain **ame** 雨; (*it rains*) **ame ga furimas'** (*furu, futte*) 雨が降る
rainy season **tsuyu** 梅雨 *or* **nyūbai** 入梅
raise **agemas'** (*ageru, agete*) 上げる
range (*kitchen*) **kamado** かまど; (*gas*) **gasu renji** ガス・レンジ
rapid *see* fast
rare (*infrequent*) **mare (na)** 稀(な); (*not cooked*) **nama no** なま; *see also* (under) done
rat **nezumi** ねずみ
rather **mushiro** むしろ
raw **nama (de)** 生(で)
razor **kamisori** かみそり
razor blade **kamisori no ha** かみそりの刃
reach *see* arrive
read **yomimas'** (*yomu, yonde*) 読む
ready **dekite imas'** *or* **dekimash'ta** 出来ている
real **hontō no** ほんとうの
really **hontō ni** ほんとうに
reason **wake** わけ *or* **riyū** 理由
receipt **uketori** 受取
receive **moraimas'** (*morau, moratte*) 貰う
recently **saikin** 最近 *or* **kono goro** 此頃
record (*phonograph*) **rekōdo** レコード
red **akai** 赤い
reduction *see* discount
refreshments (*food*) **tabemono** 食べ物;

(*drink*) **nomimono** 飲物; (*tea*) **ocha** お茶
refrigerator **reizōko** 冷蔵庫 「断る
refuse **kotowarimas'** (*kotowaru, kotowatte*)
Regards to . . . . . . **ni yorosh'ku (negaimas').** によろしく(願います)
region **chihō** 地方
registered (mail) **kaki-tome** 書留
regular **futsū no** 普通の
relation(ship) **kankei** 関係
relative **shinrui** 親類 *or* **shinseki** 親戚
religion **shūkyō** 宗教
remain **nokorimas'** (*nokoru, nokotte*) 残る; (*stay*) **imas'** (*iru, ite*) 居る *or* **ikimasen** (*ikanai, ikanai de*) 行かない 「思い出す
remember **omoi-dashimas'** (*-dasu, -dash'te*)
reminds one of **omowasemas'** (*omowaseru, omowasete*) 思わせる
remove **torimas'** (*toru, totte*) 取る
rent (*cost*) **yachin** 家賃; (*rents to*) **kashimas'** (*kasu, kash'te*) 貸す; (*rents from*) **karimas'** (*kariru, karite*) 借りる
(house for) rent **kashiya** 貸家
(rooms for) rent **kashima** 貸間
repair **naoshimas'** (*naosu, naosh'te*) 直す
repeat **mō ichido (iimas'**; *yū, itte* or *yutte*) もう一度(言う)
reporter **(shimbun-)kisha** (新聞)記者
request **negaimas'** (*negau, negatte*) 願う *or* **tanomimas'** (*tanomu, tanonde*) 頼む

require *see* need
reservation **yoyaku** 予約 *or* **mōshikomi** 申込
resign **jishoku shimas'** (*suru, sh'te*) 辞職する
respect **sonkei (shimas'**; *suru, sh'te*) 尊敬する
responsibility **sekinin** 責任
rest **yasumimas'** (*yasumu, yasunde*) 休む
rest (*remainder*) **nokori** 残り *or* **hoka** 外
restaurant **res'toran** レストラン *or* **shokudō** 食堂
restless **ochits'kanai** 落着かない
result **kekka** 結果
retail **ko-uri** 小売
retire (from business) **taishoku shimas'** (*suru, sh'te*) 退職する
return (*home*) **kaerimas'** (*kaeru, kaette*) 帰る; (*come back where one is now*) **itte kimas'** (*kuru, kite*) 行って来ます
Reverend... **...Bok'shi san** 牧師さん *or* **...Shimpu san** 神父さん
reward **hōbi** ほうび
ribbon **himo** ひも *or* **ribon** リボン
rice (*cooked*) **gohan** 御飯 *or* **meshi** 飯; (*at store*) **o-kome** お米; (*hulled*) **kome** 米; (*plants in field*) **ine** いね
rich **kanemochi** (**no**) 金持(の)
ricksha **jinrikisha** 人力車 *or* **kuruma** 車 (*but take a taxi; rickshas went out of style with Mme. Butterfly*)
ride **...ni norimas'** (*noru, notte*) *or* **...ni notte ikimas'** (*iku, itte*) に乗って行く
rifle **shōjū** 小銃

right (*not left*) **migi** 右; (*correct*) **tadashii** 正しい *or* **ii** いい
ring (*on finger*) **yubiwa** 指輪
ring (*like a bell*) **narimas'** (*naru, natte*) 鳴る
ripe **jukush'ta** 熟した
rise (*get up*) **okimas'** (*okiru, okite*) 起きる; (*go up*) **agarimas'** (*agaru, agatte*) 上がる *or* (*sun, climb*) **noborimas'** (*noboru, nobotte*) 昇る
river **kawa** 川
road **michi** 道
roast beef **rōsu(-biifu)** ロース(ビーフ)
rob *see* steal
robber **dorobō** 泥棒
rock **ishi** 石 *or* **iwa** 岩
roll **korogarimas'** (*korogaru, korogatte*) ころがる
roof **yane** 屋根
room **heya** 部屋
root **ne** 根
rope **nawa** 縄 *or* **tsuna** 綱
rose **bara** ばら
rot **k'sarimas'** (*k'saru, k'satte*) 腐る
rough **arai** 粗い
round **marui** 円い
row (a boat) **kogimas'** (*kogu, koide*) 漕ぐ
rub **kosurimas'** (*kosuru, kosutte*) 擦る
rubber **gomu** ゴム
rude **burei (na)** 無礼(な)
rug **shikimono** 敷物 or **jūtan** じゅうたん
ruin **dame ni shimas'** (*suru, sh'te*) 駄目にする

rumor **uwasa** うわさ
run **hashirimas'** (*hashiru, hashitte*) 走る *or* **kakemas'** (*kakeru, kakete*) 駆ける
rush **isogimas'** (*isogu, isoide*) 急ぐ
Russia **Roshiya** ロシヤ *or* **Soren** ソ連
rust **sabi** さび

S

sack **fukuro** 袋
sad **kanashii** 悲しい
saddle **kura** 鞍
safe(ly) **buji (ni)** 無事(に)
safety pin **anzem-pin** 安全ピン
sail **ho** 帆
sailor **funanori** 船乗り *or* **suifu** 水夫; (*member of crew*) **sen-in** 船員; (*naval enlisted man*) **suihei** 水兵
sake of . . . . . **no tame (ni)** の為(に)
saké (rice wine) **(o-)sake** (お)酒
salad **sarada** サラダ
salary **hōkyū** 俸給 *or* **kyūryō** 給料; (*monthly*) **gekkyū** 月給
saliva **tsubaki** つばき(唾)
salmon **sake** さけ(鮭)
salt **shio** 塩
same **onaji** 同じ
sample **mihon** 見本
sand **suna** 砂
sandal **sandaru** サンダル

sandwich **sando(-witchi)** サンド(ウィッチ)
sanitary **eisei-teki (na)** 衛生的(な)
sanitary belt **gekkei-tai** 月経帯
sarcasm **hiniku** 皮肉
sardine **iwashi** いわし
satin **shusu** しゅす
satisfied **manzoku shimas'** (*suru, sh'te*) 満足(する)
Saturday **doyōbi** 土曜日
sauce **sōsu** ソース
saucer **ko-zara** 小皿, **uke-zara** 受皿
save (*time, etc.*) **ken-yaku shimas'** (*suru, sh'te*) 倹約する
saw **nokogiri** のこぎり
say (that...) **(...to) iimas'** (*yū, itte or yutte*) (と)言う
scarce **s'kunai** 少い
scenery **kesh'ki** 景色
schedule (*train*) **daiya** ダイヤ; (*the timetable itself*) **jikan-hyō** 時間表
scholar **gak'sha** 学者
school **gakkō** 学校
science **kagaku** 科学
scissors **hasami** 鋏
scold **sh'karimas'** (*sh'karu, sh'katte*) 叱る
scrambled eggs **s'kuramburu-eggu** スクランブル・エッグ
scratch **kakimas'** (*kaku, kaite*) 掻く
screen (*folding*) **byōbu** びょうぶ
screw **neji** ねじ
screwdriver **neji-mawashi** ねじ回し
scroll **makimono** 巻物

sea **umi** 海

seal (*for stamping one's name*) **han** 判 *or* **in** 印

search for **sagashimas'** (*sagasu, sagash'te*) 探す

seasickness **funa-yoi** 船酔

season **kisetsu** 季節

seasoning (*food*) **chōmi** 調味 *or* **aji** 味

seat **koshi-kake** こしかけ *or* **zaseki** 座席 *or* **seki** 席

second **futatsu-me no** 二つ目の *or* **ni-bamme no** 二番目の

second class **ni-tō** 二等

secondhand **chūburu no** 中古の *or* **furui** 古い

secret **himitsu** 秘密

secretary **shoki** 書記

see **mimas'** (*miru, mite*) 見る

seed **tane** 種

seek *see* search for

seems like **. . . to miemas'** (*mieru, miete*) と見える *or* **. . . rashii des'** らしいです

seize **ts'kamimas'** (*ts'kamu, ts'kande*) つかむ *or* **toraemas'** (*toraeru, toraete*) 捕える

seldom **metta ni . . .** + NEGATIVE めったに *or* **hotondo** + NEGATIVE 殆ど

select *see* choose

self **jibun** 自分

selfish **wagamama** わがまま

sell **urimas'** (*uru, utte*) 売る

send **okurimas'** (*okuru, okutte*) 送る; (*a telegram*) **uchimas'** (*utsu, utte*) 打つ; (*a*

person) **ikasemas'** (*ikaseru, ikasete*) 行かせる
sense *see* feel
sentence (*written*) **bunshō** 文章; (*spoken*) **koto** こと
separate (*different*) **betsu (no)** 別の; (*separates them*) **wakemas'** (*wakeru, wakete*) 分ける; (*they separate*) **wakaremas'** (*wakareru, wakarete*) 分れる
September **Ku-gatsu** 九月
sergeant **gunsō** 軍曹
serious **majime (na)** まじめ(な)
servant **meshits'kai** 召使い; **shiyōnin** 使用人
serve (*a meal*) **dashimas'** (*dasu, dash'te*) 出す
service (*in restaurant, etc.*) **sābisu** サービス
sesame **goma** ごま
set **okimas'** (*oku, oite*) 置く; (*hair*) **setto** セット; *see also* sit
set (*collection*) **(hito-)kumi** (一)組
settle (*decide*) **kimemas'** (*kimeru, kimete*) 定める
seven **nana** *or* **shichi** 七 *or* **nanatsu** 七つ
seventeen **jū nana** *or* **jū shichi** 十七
seventy **nana-jū** *or* **shichi-jū** 七十
several **f'tatsu-mitsu** 二つ三つ *or* **jakkan** 若干
sew **nuimas'** (*nuu, nutte*) 縫う
sewing machine **mishin** ミシン
sex **sei** 性
(has) sex **yarimas'** (*yaru, yatte*) やる
shade **kage** 蔭
shadow **kagebōshi** 影法師

shake (*shakes it*) **furimas'** (*furu, futte*) 振る; (*it shakes*) **furuemas'** (*furueru, furuete*) 震える
shall USE PRESENT TENSE (**shimas', suru**, etc.)
shame **hazukashii koto** はずかしいこと
(That's a) shame. **Sore wa ikemasen ne.**
shape **katachi** 形
(one's) share (of expenses) **dashi-mae** 出し前; *see also* divide, Dutch
shark **same** さめ
sharp **surudoi** 鋭い
shave **hige o sorimas'** (*soru, sotte*) ひげをそる
she **kano-jo** 彼女 *or* **ano hito** あの人
shed **mono-oki** 物置
sheep **hitsuji** 羊
sheet (*of paper, etc.*) (**ichi-**)**mai** (一)枚
sheets (*for bed*) **shiitsu** シーツ
shelf **tana** 棚
shell **kara** 殻
shine (*it shines*) **hikarimas'** (*hikaru,hikatte*) 光る; (*shines it*) **migakimas'** (*migaku, migaite*) 磨く
ship **fune** 船
shirt **wai-shatsu** ワイシャツ; (*undershirt*) **shatsu** シャツ
shoe **kutsu** 靴
shoe box **geta-bako** 下駄箱
shoehorn **kutsu-bera** 靴べら
shoelaces **kutsu-himo** 靴ひも
shoeshine (man) **kutsu-migaki** 靴磨き
shoot **irimas'** (*iru, itte*) 射る
shop (*store*) **mise** 店

shopping **kai-mono** 買物
shore **kishi** 岸 *or* **kaigan** 海岸 ┌**hikui** 低い
short (*not long*) **mijikai** 短い; (*not tall*)
short cut **chika-michi** 近道
should *see* ought
shoulder **kata** 肩
shout (*call out*) **sakebimas'** (*sakebu, sakende*) 叫ぶ; (*speak londly*) **donarimas'**; (*donaru,*
shovel **shaberu** シャベル └*donatte*) 怒鳴る
show **misemas'** (*miseru, misete*) 見せる; *see also* movie, play
shower (bath) **shawā** シャワー
shrimp(s) **ebi** えび; (*fried in batter, Japanese style*) **ebi-tempura** えび天ぷら; (*fried in bread crumbs, American style*) **ebi-furai** えびフライ ┌*or* **jingū** 神宮
shrine (*Shinto*) **(o-)miya** お宮 *or* **jinja** 神社
shrink **chijimimas'** (*chijimu, chijinde*) 縮む
shut **shimemas'** (*shimeru, shimete*) 締める
shy **uchiki (na)** 内気(な); **hanikamimas'** (*hanikamu, hanikande*) はにかむ
Siberia **Shiberiya** シベリヤ
sick **byōki (no)** 病気(の); (*feels sick to one's stomach*) **mukats'kimas'** (*mukats'ku, mukatsuite*) むかつく
side **yoko** 横; *or* (*of body*) **waki** わき
(that) side **achira-gawa** あちら側
(this) side **kochira-gawa** こちら側
(which) side **dochira-gawa** どちら側

(both) sides **ryō-gawa** 両側
sidewalk **hodō** 歩道 *or* **jindō** 人道
sieve **furui** ふるい(篩)
sight-seeing **kembutsu** 見物 *or* **kankō** 観光
sign (board) **kamban** 看板 「*sh'te*) 署名する
sign (one's name) **shomei shimas'** (*suru*,
signal **shingō** 信号
silent **damarimas'** (*damaru, damatte*) 默る
silk **kinu** 絹
silver **gin** 銀
simple **kantan (na)** 簡単(な)
since **(sono) go** (その)後
sincere **seijitsu (na)** 誠実
sing **utaimas'** (*utau, utatte*) 歌う
single (*for one person*) **hitori no** 一人の; (*unmarried*) **hitori-mono** ひとりもの
sink (*in kitchen*) **nagashi** 流し; (*it sinks*) **shizumimas'** (*shizumu, shizunde*) 沈む; (*sinks it*) **shizumemas'** (*shizumeru, shizumete*) 沈める
sister **onna no kyōdai** 女のきょうだい; (*older*) **ane** 姉 *or* **nē-san** ねえさん; (*younger*) **imōto(-san)** 妹(さん)
sit **suwarimas'** (*suwaru, suwatte*) 坐る (*strictly speaking this is Japanese style, but it is used for both*); (*chair style*) **kosh'-kakemas'** (*-kakeru, -kakete*) 腰掛ける
six **roku** 六 *or* **muttsu** 六つ
sixteen **jū roku** 十六

sixty **roku-jū** 六十
size **ōkisa** 大きさ
skating **s'kēto** スケート 「(をする)
ski **s'kii (o shimas';** *suru, sh'te*) スキー
skin (*of person*) **hifu** 皮膚; (*of animal*) **kawa** 皮
skirt(s) **s'kāto** スカート; (*of mountain*) **suso** 裾
sky **sora** 空
sled **sori** そり
sleep **nemas'** (*neru, nete*) 寝る *or* **nemuri-mas'** (*nemuru, nemutte*) 眠る
sleepy **nemui** 眠い
sleeve **sode** 袖; (*end of kimono sleeve*) **tamoto** 袂
slender **hosoi** 細い
slice *see* cut; *see* piece
slide, slip **suberimas'** (*suberu, subette*) 滑る
slippers **surippa** スリッパ *or* **uwabaki** 上履
slot **kuchi** 口
slow **osoi** 遅い
sly **zurui** ずるい
small *see* little
small-size (model) **kogata** 小型
smell **nioi** におい; (*it smells*) **nioimas'** (*niou, notte*) におう *or* **nioi ga shimas'** (*suru, sh'te*) においがする; (*smells it*) **kagimas'** (*kagu, kaide*) 嗅ぐ 「にこする
smile **niko-niko shimas'** (*suru, sh'te*) にこ
smoke **kemuri** 煙; (*smokes a cigarette*) **tabako o nomimas'** (*nomu, nonde*) タバコを呑む *or* **suimas'** (*suu, sutte*) 吸う

smooth **nameraka (na)** 滑か(な) *or* **subekkoi** 滑っこい
snack **oyatsu** おやつ
snake **hebi** 蛇
sneeze **kushami (shimas'**; *suru, sh'te*) くしゃみする
snore **ibiki (o kakimas'**; *kaku, kaite*) いびき(をかく)
snow **yuki (ga furimas'**; *furu, futte*) 雪が降る
so **sō** そう; (much) **sonna ni** そんなに
soap **sekken** 石けん *or* **shabon** シャボン
socialism **shakai-shugi** 社会主義
society **shakai** 社会, (*association*) **kyōkai** 協会
socks **kutsu-sh'ta** 靴下
soft **yawarakai** 柔らかい
soil (*earth*) **tsuchi** 土 *or* **tochi** 土地; (*makes dirty*) **yogoshimas'** (*yogosu, yogosh'te*) よごす; (*gets dirty*) **yogoremas'** (*yogoreru, yogorete*) よごれる
soldier **heitai** 兵隊
solid **katai** 堅い
some (*a little*) **s'koshi** (*but often omitted in Japanese*)
some (*a particular one*) **aru...** ある; (people) **aru hito** ある人
somebody **dare ka** 誰か
something **nani ka** 何か
sometime **itsu ka** いつか
sometimes **toki-doki** 時々
somewhere **doko ka** 何処か
son **mus'ko** むすこ *or* (*someone elses*) **bot-chan** 坊っちゃん
song **uta** 歌
soon **ma-mo-naku** 間もなく *or* **sugu** すぐ

sore **itai** 痛い
sorry (*for you or him*) **ki no doku des'** 気の毒です
Sorry! **Sumimasen.** すみません
sort (*kind*) **shurui** 種類
soul *see* spirit
sound (*noise*) **oto** 音
soup **sūpu** スープ; (*Japanese clear*) **sui-mono** 吸物; (*Japanese dark*) **miso-shiru** みそ汁
soup-stock **dashi** 出し
sour **suppai** すっぱい
south **minami** 南
Soviet Union **Soren** ソ連
sow (seeds) **makimas'** (*maku, maite*) 蒔く
space (*available*) **ma** 間; (*between two things*) **aida** あいだ
Spain **S'pein** スペイン
Spanish (language) **S'pein-go** スペイン語
sparrow **suzume** すずめ
speak **hanashimas'** (*hanasu, hanash'te*) 話す
special **tokubetsu no** 特別の
special 2nd class **toku-ni** 特二 *or* **tokubetsu-nitō** 特別二等
spectacles *see* glasses
speech **hanashi** 話
speed **hayasa** 速さ *or* **sokudo** 速度
spell **ji o tsuzurimas'** (*tsuzuru, tsuzutte*) 字を綴る
spend **ts'kaimas'** (*ts'kau, ts'katte*) 使う *or* **dashimas'** (*dasu, dash'te*) 出す
spices **chōmi(-ryō)** 調味(料)
spider **kumo** くも(蜘蛛)
spill **koboshimas'** (*kobosu, kobosh'te*) こぼす

spinach **hōrensō** ほうれんそう
spinning (mill) **bōseki(-kōjō)** 紡績(工場)
spirit **seishin** 精神 *or* **kokoro** 心 「(を)吐く
spit (**tsuba o**) **hakimas'** (*haku, haite*) (つば
(in) spite of . . .(that) (**sore**). . .(**na**) **no ni** (それ
splendid **rippa** (**na**) 立派(な) 」な)のに
split (*splits it*) **warimas'** (*waru, watte*) 割る;
(*it splits*) **waremas'** (*wareru, warete*) 割れる
spoil (*spoils it*) **waruku shimas'** (*suru, sh'te*)
悪くする; (*it spoils*) **waruku narimas'**
sponge **kaimen** 海面 」(*naru, natte*) 悪くなる
spongecake **kas'tera** カステラ
spoon **s'pūn** スプーン *or* **saji** 匙
sport(s) **s'pōtsu** スポーツ *or* **undō** 運動
spot **ten** 点
spread (*spreads it*) **hirogemas'** (*hirogeru, hirogete*) 広げる; (*spreads it out*) **nobashimas'** (*nobasu, nobash'te*) 伸ばす; (*it spreads*) **hirogarimas'** (*hirogaru, hirogatte*) 広がる; (*it spreads out*) **nobimas'** (*nobiru, nobite*)
spring (*season*) **haru** 春 」伸びる
(hot) spring **onsen** 温泉
spy **s'pai** スパイ
square **sh'kaku** 四角 「しゃがむ
squat **shagamimas'** (*shagamu, shagande*)
squeeze **tsubushimas'** (*tsubusu, tsubush'te*)
つぶす; (out) **shiborimas'** (*shiboru, shibotte*)
squirrel **risu** りす 」しぼる
stage **butai** 舞台

stairs **kaidan** 階段 *or* (*wooden*) **hashigo-dan** はしご段
stamp (*postal*) **kitte** 切手
stand (up) **tachimas'** (*tatsu, tatte*) 立つ
star **hoshi** 星
start *see* begin
state (of the U.S.) **shū** 州
station (*railroad*) **eki** 駅; *see also* gas station
stationery **binsen** 便箋
statue **zō** 像 *or* (*bronze*) **dōzō** 銅像
stay **imas'** (*iru, ite*) 居る *or* **todomarimas'** (*todomaru, todomatte*) 留まる; (*over night*) **tomarimas'** (*tomaru, tomatte*) 泊まる
steal **nusumimas'** (*nusumu, nusunde*) 盗む
steam **jōki** 蒸気 *or* **yuge** 湯気
steel **hagane** はがね *or* **kōtetsu** 鋼鉄
step (*walk*) **arukimas'** (*aruku, aruite*) 歩く
stick (*club*) **bō(kkire)** 棒(っきれ); (*it sticks to*) **. . . ni kuttsukimas'** (*kuttsuku, kuttsuite*) にくっつく; (*sticks it on*) **harimas'** (*haru, hatte*) 貼る
sticky **neba-neba shimas'** (*suru, sh'te*) ねばねばする
still (*yet*) **mada** まだ; (*but*) **demo** でも
sting **sashimas'** (*sasu, sash'te*) 刺す
stir **kaki-mawashimas'** (*mawasu, mawash'te*) かき回す
stockings **kutsu-sh'ta** 靴下
stomach **o-naka** おなか *or* **hara** 腹
stone **ishi** 石
stop (*it comes to rest*) **tomarimas'** (*tomaru, tomatte*) とまる; (*it stops*) **yamimas'** (*yamu,*

yande) 止む; (*stops it*) **tomemas'** (*tomeru, tomete*) とめる; (*stops doing it*) **yamemas'** (*yameru, yamete*) 止める

store (*shop*) **mise** 店

storm **arashi** あらし(嵐)

story **hanashi** 話

stove **s'tōbu** ストーブ *or* (*kitchen*) **kamado** かまど

straight **massugu** (**na**) まっすぐ(な)

strange **hen** (**na**) 変(な)

stranger **shiranai hito** 知らない人

straw **wara** わら

strawberry **ichigo** いちご

street **michi** 道 *or* **shadō** 車道

stretch (*stretches it*) **nobashimas'** (*nobasu, nobash'te*) 伸ばす; (*it stretches*) **nobimas'** (*nobiru, nobite*) 伸びる

strike **s'toraiki** ストライキ; *see also* hit

string (*thread*) **ito** 糸; (*cord*) **himo** ひも

strong **tsuyoi** 強い

student **gak'sei** 学生

study **benkyō shimas'** (*suru, sh'te*) 勉強する

stuff (*thing*) **mono** 物; (*fill*) **tsumemas'** (*tsumeru, tsumete*) つめる

styptic pencil **chi-dome** 血止め

suburb **kōgai** 郊外

subway **chikatetsu** 地下鉄

succeed **seikō shimas'** (*suru, sh'te*) 成功する

such **sonna** そんな

suck **suimas'** (*suu, sutte*) 吸う

suddenly **totsuzen** 突然
sugar **satō** 砂糖
suit **yōf'ku** 洋服
suitable **fusawashii** ふさわしい
suitcase **kaban** かばん
summer **natsu** 夏
sun **o-hi-sama** お日さま *or* **taiyō** 太陽
sun-bathing **hinata-bokko** ひなたぼっこ
Sunday **nichiyōbi** 日曜日
sunshine **hinata** ひなた
supper **ban-gohan** 晩御飯
supply **kyōkyū shimas'** (*suru, sh'te*) 供給する
suppose *see* think
sure **tash'ka (na)** 確か(な)
surprised **bikkuri shimas'** (*suru, sh'te*) びっくりする *or* **odorokimas'** (*odoroku, odoroite*) 驚く
swallow (*bird*) **tsubame** つばめ
swan **hakuchō** はくちょう
sweat **ase** (**ga demas'**; *deru, dete*) 汗が出る
sweep **sōji shimas'** (*suru, sh'te*) 掃除する *or* **hakimas'** (*haku, haite*) 掃く
sweeper **sōji-ki** 掃除機
sweet (*taste*) **amai** 甘い
sweetheart **ii-hito** いい人 *or* **koibito** 恋人
swell up **haremas'** (*hareru, harete*) 腫る; **ōkiku narimas'** (*naru, natte*) 大きくなる
swim **oyogimas'** (*oyogu, oyoide*) 泳ぐ
swim suit *see* bathing suit

swing (back and forth) **yuremas'** (*yureru, yurete*) ゆれる
sword **katana** 刀
syllable **onsetsu** 音節
syringe (*for injections*) **chūsha-ki** 注射器; (*for water*) **chūsui-ki** 注水器
syrup **shiroppu** シロップ
system **taikei** 体系 *or* **seido** 制度

T

table **tēburu** テーブル
table-cloth **tēburu-kake** テーブル掛け
tail **shippo** しっぽ
tailor **shitate-ya** 仕立屋 *or* **yōf'ku-ya** 洋服屋
take **torimas'** (*toru, totte*) 取る
talk **hanashimas'** (*hanasu, hanash'te*) 話す
tall **takai** 高い
tangerine **mikan** みかん
tape **tēpu** テープ
tape recorder **tēpu-rekōdā** テープ・レコーダー
taste **ajiwaimas'** (*ajiwau, ajiwatte*) 味う; (*flavor*) **aji** 味
tattoo **ire-zumi** いれずみ
tax **zei** 税
taxi **tak'shii** タクシー *or* **kuruma** 車
tea **cha** 茶; (*green*) **o-cha** お茶; (*black*) **kōcha** 紅茶
teach **oshiemas'** (*oshieru, oshiete*) 教える
teacher **sensei** 先生
team **chiimu** チーム

tear (*in eye*) **namida** 涙
tear (tore, torn) **sakimas'** (*saku, saite*) 裂く
or **yaburimas'** (*yaburu, yabutte*) 破る
tease **ijimemas'** (*ijimeru, ijimete*) いじめる
telegram **dempō** (**o uchimas'**; *utsu, utte*)
電報(を打つ) 「*kakete*) 電話 (をかける)
telephone **denwa** (**o kakemas'**; *kakeru,*
television **terebi** テレビ
tell **iimas'** (*yū, itte* or *yutte*) 言う
temple (**o-**)**tera** (お)寺
ten **jū** *or* **tō** 十
tent **tento** テント 「**osoroshii** 恐しい
terrible **mono-sugoi** ものすごい; (*frightening*)
terribly **mono-sugoku** ものすごく; (*frighten-*
test **sh'ken** 試験 ⌊*ingly* **osorosh'ku** 恐しく
than . . . **. . . yori** より 「を言う
thank **o-rei o iimas'** (*yū, itte* or *yutte*) お礼
Thank you. **Arigatō** (**gozaimas'**). *or* **Dōmo.**
or **Sumimasen.** 「あの
that . . . **sono . . .** その; (*over there*) **ano . . .**
that (one) **sore** それ; (*over there*) **are** あれ
the *usually not translated* 「**shibai** 芝居
theater (*building*) **gekijō** 劇場; (*play*)
them, they (*people*) **ano hito-tachi** あの人達
or **kare-ra** 彼等; (*things*) **sore-ra** それら
then (*at that time*) **sono toki** その時; (*after*
that) **sore kara** それから; (*in that case*)
sore nara それなら 「あそこ
there **soko** そこ; (*over there*) **as'ko** *or* **asoko**

thermos bottle **mahō-bin** まほおびん

these **kore-ra** これら

they *see* them

thick **atsui** 厚い; (and round) **futoi** 太い

thief **dorobō** 泥棒

thimble **yubinuki** 指貫

thin **usui** 薄い; (and round) **hosoi** 細い

thing **mono** もの(物); (*fact*) **koto** こと(事)

think (that . . .) (**. . . to**) **omoimas'** (*omou, omotte*) (と)思う *or* **kangaemas'** (*kangaeru, kangaete*) 考える

third **mittsu-me** (**no**) 三っ目(の) *or* **sambam-me** (**no**) 三番目(の)

third class **san-tō** 三等

thirsty **nodo ga kawakimash'ta** のどがかわきました

thirteen **jū san** 十三

thirty **san-jū** 三十

this . . . **kono . . .** この

this (one) **kore** これ

thorn **toge** 刺

those *see* them

though **de mo** でも

thought **kangae** 考

thousand **sen** 千

thousand Yen **sen-en** 千円

thread **ito** 糸

three **san** 三 *or* **mittsu** 三つ

throat **nodo** のど

through (*putting*) **. . . o tōsh'te** を通して; (*coming*) **. . . o tōtte** 通って; (*seeing*) . . .

(no aida) **kara** (の間)から; (*by means of*) ...**de** で *or* ...**o ts'katte** を使って

through (*finished*) ...**te shimaimash'ta** しまいました *or* **dekimash'ta** 出来ました

throw **nagemas'** (*nageru, nagete*) 投げる

thumb **oya-yubi** 親指

thunder **kaminari** かみなり

Thursday **mokuyōbi** 木曜日

ticket **kippu** 切符

ticket seller **kippu-uri** 切符売り

tickle **kusugurimas'** (*kusuguru, kusugutte*) くすぐる

tide **shio** 潮

tie **musubimas'** (*musubu, musunde*) 結ぶ; *see also* necktie

tiger **tora** 虎

tight **kitsui** きつい, **katai** 堅い; (*skimpy*) **semai** 狭い; *see also* drunk

tile (*roof*) **kawara** 瓦; (*floor*) **tairu** タイル

time **toki** 時; (*hour*) **jikan** 時間; (*free*) **hima** ひま

tin **buriki** ブリキ

tip (*money*) **chippu** チップ *or* **kokorozuke** 心付け

tire (*of wheel*) **taiya** タイヤ

(gets) tired **ts'karemas'** (*ts'kareru, ts'karete*) 疲れる

to ...**ni** に *or* ...**e** へ

tobacco **tabako** タバコ

today **kyō** 今日

toe **ashi-yubi** 足指

together **issho ni** 一緒に *or* **tomo ni** 供に

toilet **benjo** 便所

tomorrow **ash'ta** 明日

tongs (*for fire*) **hi-bashi** 火ばし

tongue **sh'ta** 舌
tonight **komban** 今晩
too (*also*) **...mo** も
too (*overly*) **ammari** あんまり
tool **dōgu** 道具
tooth **ha** 歯
tooth brush **ha-burashi** 歯ブラシ
toothpaste (*or* powder) **ha-migaki** 歯磨
toothpick **koyōji** 小楊子
top **ue** 上; (*summit*) **chōjō** 頂上
top (*toy*) **koma** こま
toss *see* throw
total **zembu** (**de**) 全部(で)
touch **sawarimas'** (*sawaru, sawatte*) 触る *or* (**te o**) **furemas'** (*fureru, furete*) (手を)触れる
tough **katai** 堅い
tourist **kankō-kyaku** 観光客
toward **...no hō e** の方へ
towel **tenugui** 手拭 *or* **taoru** タオル
town **machi** 町
toy **omocha** おもちゃ
trader **shōnin** 商人
traffic **kōtsū** 交通
traffic signal(s) **kōtsū-shingō** 交通信号
train **kisha** 汽車; (*electric*) **densha** 電車
translate **yakushimas'** (*yakusu, yakush'te*) 訳す
travel **ryokō shimas'** (*suru, sh'te*) 旅行する
tray **obon** お盆

treasure **takara**(**mono**) 宝(物)
treat (*to food*) **gochisō** (**shimas'**; *suru, sh'te*) ごちそう(する); (*medically*) **chiryō shimas'** (*suru, sh'te*) 治療する
tree **ki** 木
trick *see* cheat
trip **ryokō** 旅行
trivial *see* unimportant
trouble (*inconvenience*) **tekazu** *or* **tesū** 手数 *or* **meiwaku** 迷惑 *or* **sewa** 世話; (*difficulty*) **konnan** 困難 *or* **komaru tokoro** 困るところ; *see also* worry
trousers **zubon** ズボン
trout **masu** ます (鱒)
truck **torakku** トラック; (*3-wheeled*) **sanrin-sha** 三輪車
true **honto** (**no**) ほんと(の)
truly **honto ni** ほんとに *or* **makoto ni** まことに
trust **shin-yō shimas'** (*suru, sh'te*) 信用する
try **yatte mimas'** (*miru, mite*) やってみる
tub **oke** 桶
tube **kuda** *or* **kan** 管
tuberculosis **kekkaku** 結核 *or* **haibyō** 肺病
Tuesday **kayōbi** 火曜日
tunnel **tonneru** トンネル
Turkey **Toruko** トルコ
turkey **shichimen-chō** しちめんちょう
turn (*change directions*) **magarimas'** (*magaru, magatte*) 曲る; (*go round*) **mawarimas'** (*mawaru, mawatte*) 回る; (*make go round*) **mawashimas'** (*mawasu, mawash'te*) 回す
turtle **kame** かめ (亀)

twelve **jū ni** 十二
twenty **ni-jū** 二十
twice (*two times*) **ni-do** 二度 *or* **ni-kai** 二回; (*double*) **ni-bai** 二倍
twins **f'tago** ふたご
two **ni** 二 *or* **f'tatsu** 二つ; (*people*) **f'tari** 二人
type(write) **taipu(raitā) de uchimas'** (*utsu, utte*) タイプ(ライター) で打つ
typewriter **taipuraitā** タイプライター
typhoon **taifū** 大風

U

ugly **minikui** 醜い
umbrella **kasa** 傘
unbutton **botan o hazushimas'** (*hazusu, hazush'te*) ボタンをはずす
uncle **oji san** おじさん
uncomfortable **furaku** (**na**) 不樂(な)
unconcerned *see* calm
under **...no sh'ta** (**ni**) の下 (に)
understand **wakarimas'** (*wakaru, wakatte*) わかる
underwear **sh'ta-gi** 下着
undo **hazushimas'** (*hazusu, hazush'te*) はずす
undress **kimono o nugimas'** (*nugu, nuide*) 着物を脱ぐ
uniform **seif'ku** 制服
unimportant (*matter*) **mondai ni naranai** 問題にならない
unless **...(shi-)nakereba** (し)なければ
untie **tokimas'** (*toku, toite*) 解く *or* **hodoki-**

mas' (*hodoku, hodoite*) ほどく
until . . . **made** まで
unusual **kawatta** 変った
up (. . . **no**) **ue e** 上へ
(go) up **agarimas'** (*agaru, agatte*) 上る
upon *see* on 「あべこべ
upside down **sakasama** さかさま *or* **abekobe**
upstairs (**o-**)**nikai** (**ni**) (お)二階(に) 「勧める
urge **susumemas'** (*susumeru, susumete*)
urinal (*place*) **benjo** 便所; (*thing*) **shibin** 尿瓶
urinate **shōben shimas'** (*suru, sh'te*)小便する
urine **shōben** 小便
us, we **watashi-tachi** 私達
use **ts'kaimas'** (*ts'kau, ts'katte*) 使う
used to PAST (**sh'ta**)+**mon' des'**
usual **futsū no** 普通の

V

vacant **aite imas'** (*iru, ite*) あいている
vacation **yasumi** 休み
vacuum cleaner **shinkū-sōjiki** 真空掃除機
vague **aimai** (**na**) あいまい(な)
valley **tani**(**ma**) 谷間
valuable **taisetsu** (**na**) 大切(な)
value **neuchi** 値打
valve **ben** 弁
vanish (*from sight*) **mienaku narimas'** (*naru, natte*) 見えなくなる; (*from ex-*

istence) **naku narimas'** (*naru, natte*) 無くなる

various **iroiro (no/na)** 色々 (の/な)*or* **ironna** 「いろんな

vase **bin** びん; (*for flowers*) **kabin** 花びん

vegetable **yasai** 野菜

vehicle **norimono** 乗物 *or* **kuruma** 車

velvet **birōdo** ビロード

venereal disease **seibyō** 性病

verb **dōshi** 動詞

very **taihen** 大変 *or* **hijō ni** 非常に

vest **chokki** チョッキ

view *see* opinion; *see* scenery; *see* look

village **mura** 村

vinegar **su** 酢

violet **sumire** すみれ

virgin (*woman*) **oboko** おぼこ *or* **shojo** 処女; (*man*) **dōtei** 童貞

visit **asobi ni ikimas'** (*iku, itte*) 遊びに行く *or* **tazunemas'** (*tazuneru, tazunete*) 尋ねる *or* **ukagaimas'** (*ukagau, ukagatte*) 伺う

visitor **raikyaku** 来客

vitamin(s) **bitamin** ビタミン

vocabulary **kotoba** ことば *or* **goi** 語彙

voice **koe** 声

volcano **kazan** 火山

vomit **modoshimas'** (*modosu, modosh'te*) もどす

vote **tōhyō shimas'** (*suru, sh'te*) 投票する

vulgar **gehin (na)** 下品(な)

W

waist **koshi** 腰
wait **machimas'** (*matsu, matte*) 待つ
waiter, waitress **kyūji** 給仕
waiting room **machiai-shitsu** 待合室
waitress **jokyū** 女給
Waitress! **Nē-san!** *or* **Chotto!**
wake up **me ga samemas'** (*sameru, samete*) 目がさめる; (*someone*) **...o okoshimas'** (*okosu, okosh'te*) を起す
walk **arukimas'** (*aruku, aruite*) 歩く; (*takes a*) **sampo shimas'** (*suru, sh'te*) 散歩する
wall (*of house*) **kabe** 壁; (*around courtyard, etc.*) **hei** 塀
wallet **saifu** 財布 *or* **satsu-ire** 礼入れ *or* **gamaguchi** がまぐち
wander **samayoimas'** (*samayou, samayotte*) さまよう
want (**...ga**) **irimas'** (*iru, itte*) 要る
war **sensō** 戦争
warm **attakai** (*or* **atatakai**) 暖い; (*lukewarm liquids*) **nurui** ぬるい
was *see* is
wash **araimas'** (*arau, aratte*) 洗う; (*launder*) **sentaku shimas'** (*suru, sh'te*) 洗濯する
washcloth **f'kin** ふきん
washer **sentak'-ki** 洗濯機
washing **sentaku** *or* **sentaku-mono** 洗濯(物)

washroom **o-tearai** お手洗 「する
waste **muda ni shimas'** (*suru, sh'te*) むだに
weigh (**. . . no**) **mekata o hakarimas'** (*ha-karu, hakatte*) (の)目方を計る
wastebasket (**kami**)**kuzu-kago** (紙)くずかご
watch **tokei** 時計; *see also* look
water **mizu** 水
waterfall **taki** 滝
watermelon **suika** すいか
water pistol **mizu-deppō** 水鉄砲
waterproof **bōsui** (**no**) 防水(の)
wave **nami** 波
wax (**mitsu**)**rō** (蜜) 蠟 「**yarikata** やりかた
way **michi** 道; (*method*) **sh'kata** 仕方 *or*
(gets in the) way **jama ni narimas'** (*naru, natte*) *or* **jama o shimas'** (*suru, sh'te*) じゃまになる *or* じゃまをする 「退く
(gets out of the) way **dokimas'** (*doku, doite*)
we *see* us
weak **yowai** 弱い
wealthy *see* rich
wear (*on body*) **kimas'** (*kiru, kite*) 着る; (*on legs or feet*) **hakimas'** (*haku, haite*) はく; (*on head*) **kaburimas'** (*kaburu, kabutte*) かぶる; (*on hands*) **hamemas'** (*hameru*
weather **tenki** 天気 ⌊*hamete*) はめる
weather forecast **tenki-yohō** 天気予報
weave **orimas'** (*oru, otte*) 織る
wedding **kekkon**(**-sh'ki**) 結婚(式)

Wednesday **suiyōbi** 水曜日
weed **zassō** 雑草
week **shūkan** 週間
weep **nakimas'** (*naku, naite*) 泣く
weight **mekata** 目方 *or* **omosa** 重さ
Welcome! **Yoku irasshaimash'ta!** *or* **Yō koso!**
Welcome home. **O-kaeri nasai.**
(You're) welcome. **Dō itashimash'te.**
well (*for water*) **ido** 井戸
well (*good*) **yoku** よく
were *see* is
west **nishi** 西
wet **nureta** ぬれた
whale **kujira** くじら
what **nani** 何 (*pronounced* **nan** *before* **t, d,** *or* **n**)
wheat **komugi** 小麦
wheel **wa** 輪 *or* **sharin** 車輪
when? **itsu** いつ
when . . . . . . (**suru**) **to** (する) と *or* . . . (**sh'-**) **tara** (し)たら *or* . . . (**sh'ta**) **toki** (した)時
where? **doko** 何処
whether . . . **ka dō ka** かどうか
which (*of two*) **dochira** どちら *or* **dotchi** どっち; (*of more than two*) **dore** どれ
while **aida** 間
whip **muchi** (**de uchimas'**; *utsu, utte*) 鞭(で打つ)
whisper **sasayakimas'** (*sasayaku, sasayaite*) 囁く *or* **mimiuchi shimas'** (*suru, sh'te*) 耳打する

whistle **fue** 笛; (*with lips*) **kuchi-bue** (**o f'kimas'**; *f'ku, fuite*) 口笛(を吹く)
white **shiroi** 白い
who? **dare** 誰
whole **zentai** (**no**) 全体(の)
wholesale **oroshi** (**de**) 卸(で)
whore *see* prostitute
whose **dare no** 誰の
why **dō sh'te** どうして *or* **naze** なぜ
wide **hiroi** 広い
widow **yamome** やもめ *or* **mibōjin** 未亡人
wife **ok'san** 奥さん; (*one's own*) **kanai** 家内
wild (*disorderly*) **rambō** (**na**) 乱暴(な); (*rough*) **arai** 粗い; (*roughneck*) **abaremono** 暴れもの; (*not cultivated*) **yama no...** 山の *or* **yasei no...** 野生の
will *see* shall
willow **yanagi** 柳
win **kachimas'** (*katsu, katte*) 勝つ
wind (*breeze*) **kaze** 風
wind (up) **makimas'** (*maku, maite*) 巻く
window **mado** 窓
wine **budō-shu** ぶどう酒
wing (*of bird or plane*) **tsubasa** 翼; (*of insect*) **hane** 羽
wink **mabataki** (**shimas'**; *suru, sh'te*) まばたき(する)
winter **fuyu** 冬
wipe **f'kimas'** (*f'ku, fuite*) 拭く
wire **harigane** 針金; *see also* telegram
wise **kash'koi** 賢い
wish for **...ga hoshii** がほしい

wish to **...(sh')-tai des'** (し)たいです
with **...to** と *or* **...to issho ni** と一緒に
without (*excluding*) **...no hoka ni** の外に; (*not having*) **...ga nai to** がないと
wolf **ōkami** おおかみ
woman **onna** 女
(I) wonder ... **...ka shira.** かしら
wonderful **subarashii** すばらしい *or* **s'teki (na)** すてき(な)
wood **ki** 木 *or* **mokuzai** 木材
wood-block print **mokuhanga** 木版画
wooden shoes **geta** 下駄
woods *see* forest
wool **yōmo** 羊毛 *or* **keito** 毛糸
word **kotoba** ことば *or* **tango** 単語
work **hatarakimas'** (*hataraku, hataraite*) 働く *or* **shigoto (o shimas'**; *suru, sh'te*) 仕事(をする)
worker **shokkō** 職工 *or* **rōdōsha** 労働者
world **sekai** 世界
worm **mushi** 虫
worry **shimpai (shimas'**; *suru, sh'te*) 心配(する)
worse **motto warui** もっと悪い
worst **ichiban warui** 一ばん悪い
worth *see* value
would *see* perhaps
wrap **tsutsumimas'** (*tsutsumu, tsutsunde*) 包む
wreck (*car*) **jiko** 事故 *or* **shōtotsu** 衝突
wrestling **resuringu** レスリング; (*profes-*

sional) **puro-resu** プロ・レス; (*Japanese style*) **sumō** すもう
wrinkle **shiwa** しわ
write **kakimas'** (*kaku, kaite*) 書く
wrong (*mistaken*) **machigatta** 間違つた

Y

yard **niwa** 庭
yawn **akubi o shimas'** (*suru, sh'te*) あくびをする
year **toshi** *or* **-nen** 年
yell *see* shout
yellow **kiiroi** 黄色い
yes **hai** はい *or* **ē** ええ
yesterday **kinō** 昨日
yet **mada** まだ
you **anta** あんた *or* **anata** あなた
you all **mina san** 皆さん *or* **anta-tachi** あんたたち
young **wakai** 若い
your(s) **anta no** あんたの
youth (*young man*) **seinen** 青年

Z

zero **rei** 零; (*written symbol*) **maru** 0
zipper **chakku** チヤック *or* **jippā** ジッパー
zone **chitai** 地帯 *or* **kuiki** 区域
zoo **dōbutsuen** 動物園

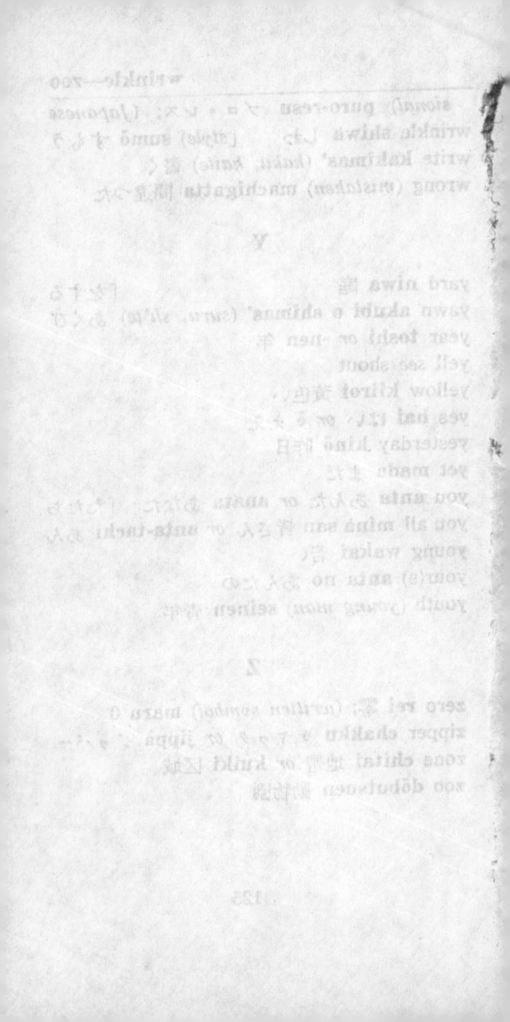

PART II

Japanese-English

NOTE: Verbs are given in both the polite present (**-mas'**) and the plain present (**-u**). Where these two forms would be at about the same place in alphabetical order, they are given together; when they are rather different in shape, you will find two entries. Occasionally a word is out of alphabetical order for convenience, but not more than a place or two. If you do not find the word you are looking for, glance up and down the page a bit. Note that **f'** is alphabetized as **fu**, **ts'** as **tsu**, **s'** as **su**, etc.; **sh'** is alphabetized as **shi**, and **ch'** as **chi**.

A

abekku a couple (on a date), a date
abunai dangerous
abura oil, fat, grease
agarimas', agaru goes up
agemas', ageru raises up ; gives
aida interval ; between ; while
aimas' (au) meets ; sees (a person)
ainiku unfortunately
aisatsu greeting
aite the other fellow (companion; adversary)
aitsu that one over there
ajā, ajappā well, I'll be...!
aji taste
aka-chan baby
akai red
akabō redcap
akambō baby
akarui bright, light
akemas', akeru opens ; leaves empty
aki autumn, fall
akimas', aku is open ; is empty
amai sweet
ame[1] rain
ame[2] candy
ami net
ammari too much, overly

ana hole
anata you
ane older sister
ani older brother
ano that (over there)
anshin shimas' (suru) doesn't worry, relaxes (one's anxieties)
anta you
aoi blue ; green
arai rough, coarse
araimas', arau washes
aratamemas', aratameru changes, alters, corrects
arawaremas', arawareru appears, shows up, comes out
are that one (over there)
ari ant
arigato (gozaimas') thank you
arimas', aru[1] there is ; we've got
arimash'ta there was ; we had
aru[2] a certain
arubaito a side job, a sideline
arui-wa or else, maybe
arukimas', aruku walks
asa morning
asai shallow
ase sweat
ashi foot ; leg
asobi fun ; a game ; a visit
asobimas', asobu has fun ; plays ; visits
asoko, as'ko (that place) over there
atama head

atarashii new
atarimas', **ataru** hits, faces; applies; is correct
at(a)takai warm
atemas', **ateru** guesses; hits; sets aside, appropriates, designates; touches; addresses
atena address
ato after(wards), later
atsui[1] hot
atsui[2] thick
atsumarimas', **atsumaru** meet, assemble
atsumemas', **atsumeru** collects, gathers
au (**aimas'**) meets, sees (a person)
awasemas', **awaseru** puts together, combines
azarashi seal (*animal*)
azukemas', **azukeru** entrusts, checks, deposits

B

-ba place
baai, **bawai** situation, case, circumstance
bai double
baka fool, idiot, stupid
ban[1] guard, watch; number
ban[2] evening
basho place
basu 1. bus 2. bath
batā butter
Beikoku America

beni rouge
benjo toilet
benkyō study
benri handy, convenient
bentō (box) lunch
betsu separate, special, particular
bin bottle ; jar
bōi boy, waiter, steward, clerk
boku I, me (man speaking)
bokushi minister, pastor ; Reverend
bōshi hat
botan button
bōzu Buddhist monk or priest
bu part, division, section
budō grapes
budō-shu wine
bumpō grammar
bun part, portion, share ; state, status
bungo literary language
bunka culture
bunshō (written) sentence
buta pig
buta-niku pork
byōin hospital
byōki sick ; sickness

C

cha tea

chadai tip
chakku zipper
champon alternating, skipping back and forth, mixing one's drinks (as beer and saké)
chi blood
chichi[1] father
chichi[2] breasts; mother's milk
chigaimas', chigau is different; is wrong; isn't like that
chihō area, region
chiisai, chiisa-na little, small
chiizu cheese
chika subway; underground; basement
chikai near, close by
chika-michi short cut
chikki[1] check, receipt, stub
chikki[2] stick hair-grease
chikuonki phonograph
chippu tip
chiri geography
chiri-gami Japanese Kleenex and toilet paper
chizu map
chō[1] block of a city
chō[2] head, chief, leader
chōdai please; I (humbly) take
chokki vest
chokusetsu direct
chō-kyori long distance
chōsa examination, investigation, inquiry
Chōsen Korea

chotto just a little ; just a minute
chū middle , medium
chūgakkō middle school (junior high school)
chūgata medium-size (model)
Chūgoku China
chūi[1] attention
chūi[2] 1st lieutenant ; lieutenant j. g.
chūshin center

D

da (**des'**) is ; it is
da ga but
dai- big
dai-(**ichi**) number (one)
daiben bowel movement
daigaku college, university
daiji important, precious
daijōbu OK, all right ; safe and sound ; no need to worry
daiku carpenter
daitai in general, on the whole, approximately, almost
da kara (**sa**) and so ; therefore ; that's why
dakimas', **daku** holds in the arms
damarimas', **damaru** is silent ; shuts up
damashimas', **damasu** deceives
dambō heating (in a house)
dame no good, no use, won't do ; don't !

dandan gradually
danna (san) master of the house; husband
dantai organization, group
dare who
dare ka somebody
dare mo everybody; nobody
dashi soup-stock
dashimas', dasu puts out; produces; spends; mails; begins
da tte but
de[1] (happening) at, in, on; with, by (means of)
de[2] is and; being, its being; with (its being)
de gozaimas' = de
deguchi exit
dekigoto happening, accident
dekimas', dekiru can, is possible; is produced; is finished, ready
dekimono swelling, sore, boil, pimple
demas', deru goes out, comes out, leaves, starts
dembu buttocks, hips
de mo but, however, even so
dempō telegram
denki electricity; lights
densha electric car (streetcar or elevated)
dentō 1. lamp, light, flashlight 2. tradition, convention
denwa telephone (call)
depāto department store
deru (demas') goes out, comes out, leaves, starts
desh'ta was; it was

deshō probably, probably is, it probably is
des', da is ; it is ; it is a case of . . .
de wa (**=ja**) well then ; in that case ; and so ; and now
dō how, why ; (in) what (way)
doa door
dochira which one
dochira ka either one of the two
dochira mo either one ; neither one ; both
Doitsu Germany
doitsu which one
dokimas' (**doku**) gets out of the way
doko where
doko ka somewhere
doko mo everywhere ; nowhere
doku[1] poison
doku[2] (**dokimas'**) gets out of the way
donna what kind of
dōmo 1. thank you 2. excuse me 3. ever so much
dono which
dore which one
doro mud
dorobō thief, robber
doru dollar
dō-sh'te why ; how
dotchi = dochira
dotera padded bathrobe
doyōbi Saturday
dōzo please

E

e picture
ē yes
ebi shrimp; lobster
eda branch
e-hagaki picture postcard
e-hon picture book
eiga (-kan) movie (theater)
Eigo English
Eikoku England
eisei hygiene, health, sanitation
eki railroad station
en Yen
empitsu pencil
enkai party
ensoku picnic, outing
entotsu chimney, smokestack
erabimas', erabu chooses, selects, elects
erai great, superior

F

fu an urban prefecture (Kyoto or Osaka)
fū appearance, air; way, fashion, manner
fuben inconvenient, unhandy
fuchūi carelessness
fuda label, tag, card, check

fude writing brush
fudōsan real estate
fūfu husband and wife, Mr. and Mrs.
fuhei discontent, grumbling
fuhō illegal
fui suddenly
fujin lady
fu-jiyū inconvenient : needy : weak
fukai, f'kai deep
fukimas', f'kimas' see **fuku, f'ku**
fukin, f'kin napkin, towel, cloth
fuku, f'ku[1] 1. blows 2. wipes
fuku, f'ku[2] clothes, suit, dress
fukuro, f'kuro bag, sack
fukushū, f'kushū review
fukuzatsu, f'kuzatsu complicated
fuman discontented, dissatisfied
fumei unknown, obscure
fumimas', fumu steps on
fun minute
funayoi seasick(ness)
fundoshi a loincloth, a jockstrap
fune boat
fun-iki atmosphere
Furansu France
furemas', fureru touches, comes in contact with
furi manner, air, pretense
furimas', furu[1] precipitates (rains, snows)
furimas', furu[2] waves, shakes, wags

furo bath
furōnin vagabond, tramp
furoshiki, furosh'ki a cloth wrapper
furu second-hand
furui old
furyō bad, no good
fūryū elegant
fusagimas', fusagu stops up, closes, blocks
fusawasnii suitable, worthy ; becoming
fusegimas', fusegu prevents ; defends, protects
fushigi strange ; wonderful ; suspicious
fusoku shortage, deficiency, scarcity
fusuma opaque sliding door
futa, f'ta lid
futari, f'tari two persons
futatsu, f'tatsu two; two years old; 2nd day
futo, f'to unexpectedly
futoi, f'toi fat, plump
futon, f'ton Japanese padded quilt
futsuka two days
fuyu winter

G

ga[1] SUBJECT PARTICLE (*shows the actor :* who does, what is)
ga[2] but ; and
gai damage, harm, injury
gaijin foreigner (usually American or European)

gaikō-kan diplomat
gaikoku abroad ; foreign countries
Gaimu-shō Ministry of Foreign Affairs
gakkō school
gaku learning, study, science
gakumon knowledge, learning, education
gakusei, gak'sei student, schoolboy
gakusha, gak'sha scholar
gamaguchi purse, pocketbook, wallet
gaman shimas' is patient, puts up with
gaman dekimasen (**dekinai**) can't stand it
gan-yaku a pill
garasu glass
gasorin gasoline
gasorin-sutando (**-s'tando**) filling station
gasu, gas' gas
gasu-dai gas bill
gehin vulgar
gei arts, accomplishments ; tricks, stunts
geijutsu art(s)
geisha a geisha girl
geki play, drama
gekijō theater
gekkyū monthly salary
gemmai unpolished rice
gemmitsu strict
gendai modern, up-to-date
gengo language
gen-in cause, origin, root

genki in good spirits, healthy, cheerful, vigorous
genkin, gen-nama cash, ready money
genshi(-bakudan) atom (bomb)
genzai the present (time)
genzō shimas' develops (film)
geppu monthly instalments
geri diarrhea
geri-dome anti-diarrhetic, paregoric
geshuku lodgings; board and room
-getsu month
getsuyōbi Monday
gikai the Japanese Diet (Congress)
gimon question, doubt
gimu duty, obligation
gin silver
ginkō bank
giri obligation, sense of obligation, honor
go 1. five 2. checkers
-go language
gofuku-ya dry goods store
gogatsu May
gogo P.M., afternoon
gohan cooked rice: meal; food
go-jū fifty
Gokigen yō! 1. Goodbye 2. Hello
goku very, exceedingly
Gomen kudasai! Hello—anybody home?
Gomen nasai. Excuse me.

gomi trash, rubbish, dust
gomu rubber
goran ... (you) look, see, try
Goshimpai naku! Don't worry about it.
go-yō your business
gozaimas' = arimas'
guai condition, shape, feelings (of health)
gumpuku military uniform
gun army, troops
gunjin soldier, military man
gunsō sergeant
guntai troops, army
gunzoku civilian attached to the army, D.A.C.
gutai-teki concrete, substantial, tangible, material
gūzen accidentally
gyaku opposite, contrary
gyofu fisherman
gyōgi behavior, manners
gyūniku beef
gyūnyū milk

H

ha tooth
haba width
habukimas', habuku cuts out, reduces, saves, eliminates, omits
hachi[1] eight
hachi[2] bowl, basin
hachi[3] **(mitsu-bachi)** bee

hachi-jū eighty
hadaka naked
hadashi barefoot
hae housefly
hagaki postcard
hage bald
hageshii violent, severe
haha mother
hai[1] yes
hai[2] ashes
hai[3] cupful
haibyō TB
hai-iro gray
haikara fashionable, high-class
hairimas', hairu enters; is inside
haitte imas' is inside
haitatsu delivery
haiyū actor
hajimarimas', hajimaru it begins (starts)
hajime the beginning; in the beginning
hajimete for the first time
hajimemas', hajimeru begins (starts) it
Hajimemash'te. How do you do. (on being introduced)
hakari measuring scales
hakarimas', hakaru measures, weighs
hakimas' (haku) 1. vomits, spits out 2. sweeps 3. wears on feet
hakkiri plainly, clearly, distinctly

hakkō publication
hako box
hakobimas', hakobu carries, conveys
haku 1. vomits, spits out 2. sweeps 3. wears on feet
hama beach
hambun half
hamemas', hameru wears (on fingers)
ha-migaki dentifrice, toothpaste, toothpowder
han[1] half
han[2] a seal (to stamp one's name with)
hana[1] flower
hana[2] nose
hanabi fireworks
hanagata a star (in a theatrical production)
hanao thong (on geta)
hanaremas', hanareru separates, becomes distant
hanashi talk, story, tale
hanashimas', hanasu speaks, talks; lets loose, lets go, sets free
hane feather; wing
han-i scope, range
hantai opposite, contrary, reverse
hantō peninsula
happa leaf
hara[1] belly, stomach
hara[2] field
haraimas', harau 1. pays 2. brushes aside, shakes out
haremas', hareru 1. (weather) clears up 2. swells up
hari needle; hand (of clock)

harimas', haru sticks on, pastes; spreads, stretches
haru springtime
hasami scissors, clippers
hashi[1] bridge
hashi[2] **(o-hashi)** chopsticks
hashigo ladder, stairs
hashirimas', hashiru runs
hasu oblique, slanting
hata flag
hatake field
hataki duster
hatakimas', hataku slap, beat; dust
hatarakimas', hataraku works
hato pigeon, dove
hatoba pier, wharf
hatsumei invention
hatsuon pronunciation
hattatsu development
hayai, hayaku fast, quick
hayarimas', hayaru is popular, is in fashion
hayashi[1] forest
hayashi[2] hash
hazu is expected to; is supposed to; is reasonable to expect
hazukashii ashamed
hazumimas', hazumu bounces back; cheers
hazuremas', hazureru gets disconnected, comes off, misses, fails
hazushimas', hazusu disconnects, takes off, leaves one's seat
he flatulence

hebi snake
hedatarimas', hedataru is distant, is estranged
hedatemas', hedateru separates them, estranges them, gets them apart
hedo vomit
hei wall, fence
heiki calm, composed, cool, indifferent
heikin average
heitai soldier
heiwa peace
heizei usually, ordinarily, generally
hekomimas', hekomu gets hollow, depressed
hema bungle, mess
hen[1] **(na)** strange, odd, queer
hen[2] vicinity, neighborhood
henji answer
henka change
herashimas', he-rasu decreases, cuts it down, shortens, curtails
heri border, edge
herimas', heru goes down, decreases, dwindles
heso navel, bellybutton
heta unskilful, poor, inexpert
heya room
hi[1] fire
hi[2] 1. day 2. sun
hibachi charcoal brazier
hibikimas', hibiku echoes, resounds
hidari left
hidoi severe, unreasonable, terrible
hidoku hard, cruelly, terribly

hiemas', hieru gets cold
higashi east
hige beard, mustache
higeki tragedy
hiji elbow
hijō emergency
hijō ni extremely
hikaku comparison
hikarimas', hikaru shines
hiki- VERB PREFIX ("pull and" or "take and")
hikidashi drawer
hiki-kaemasu, -kaeru exchanges, converts
hikimas' (hiku) pulls (out); draws; drags; catches; attracts; subtracts; deducts; looks up a word
hikkoshimas', hikkosu moves (one's residence)
hikōjō airport
hikōki airplane
hikō-yūbin airmail
hikui low, short
hima time; leisure, spare time; furlough, leave; dismissal (of servant); slow (business)
himitsu secret, mystery
himo string, cord, tape, strap
hin quality; elegance, refinement, dignity
hinan blame, censure, reproach
hinerimas', hineru twists
hiniku sarcasm; sarcastic; cynical
hinshitsu quality

hi-oi awning, sunshade, blind ⌈takes
hipparimas', hipparu pulls, drags, tugs at,
hiragana the roundish Japanese letters
hirakimas', hiraku opens up
hirattai flat
Hirippin Philippines
hiroba a square, a plaza, an open space
hiroi wide, broad
hiroimas', hirou picks up
hiru daytime ; noon
hiru kara afternoon
hiru-ma daytime
hisashi-buri ni after a long time (of absence)
hitai forehead, brow
hitei shimas' denies
hito person, man
hito- one
hitori one person
hitoshii equal, identical, similar
hitotsu one ; one year old ; one and the same
hitsuji sheep
hitsuyō necessity, need ; necessary
hiya (o-hiya) cold water
hiyashimas', hiyasu cools it off; refrigerates
hiyō cost, expense
hiyori weather ; conditions
hiza knee, lap
hizuke date
hō[1] alternative ; one (of two); direction, way

hō[2] law ; rule ; method
hōbi (**go-hōbi**) prize, reward
hōbō everywhere, all over, every which way
hodo extent ; limits ; moderation ; approximate time ; (not) so much as ; the more...
hodokimas', hodoku undoes, unties
hoka other, in addition to, other than
hoken insurance
hokkyoku North Pole, Arctic
hokori[1] pride, boast
hokori[2] dust
hoku- north-
hōkyū pay, salary
hombu central office
hōmen direction, quarter, district
homemas', homeru praises
hommono the real thing
hōmon call, visit
hon book
hon- main ; chief ; this ; the ; present
hondō the main route
hone bone
honki serious, earnest
honno a slight, just a little, a mere
honrai originally, from the start
hontō, honto true ; truth ; really
hon-yaku translation
hoppeta cheek
hoppō north

Hora! Huh?! What's that?! Look at that!
hora[1] cave
hora[2] trumpet-shell; exaggerration ⌈to
horemas', horeru falls in love, takes a fancy
hori ditch, moat
horidashi-mono a bargain, a real find
hōritsu law
horiwari canal
horimas', horu digs, excavates
hoshi star
hoshi-(gaki) dried (persimmons)
hoshii is desired; desires, wants
hoshimas', hosu dries it
hoshō guarantee
hōsō (-kyoku) broadcast (station)
hosoi slender
hosu (hoshimas') dries it
hōtai bandage
hoteru hotel
Hotoke-sama Buddha
hotondo almost (all); almost all the time
hyaku hundred
hyaku-man million
hyakushō farmer
hyō table, schedule
hyōban reputation, fame
hyōgen expression (words)
hyōgu-ya paper-hanger, paper repairman
hyōjō expression (on face)

hyōjun standard
hyōjun-go standard Japanese
hyōmen surface
hyotto accidentally, by chance
hyotto sh'tara maybe, possibly
hyūzu fuse

I

i- medicine, doctoring
ian consolation ; recreation
ichi[1] one
ichi[2] **(ichi-ba)** market, marketplace
ichi[3] position
ichiban number one ; first ; best ; most
ichibu a part, portion
ichido one time
ichijirushii conspicuous, prominent, striking
ichijitsu one day ; some day
ichimai a sheet ; one
ido a well
ie a house
igai unexpected
igaku medicine, medical studies
. . . igo afterwards, from ... on
ii good
ii(-) (infinitive of **yū** "saying")
iie no
iimas', yū says

iimash'ta said
iin committee (member)
iin-kai committee
ii-wake explanation, excuse
iji temper, disposition
. . . ijō above, upwards of ...
ijō unusual
. . . ika below, less than ...
ika medical department
ikada raft
ikaga how (about it)?
ikagawashii suspicious, questionable, shady
ikari anger
ike pond
ikebana flower arrangement
ikemasen, ikenai it won't do; you mustn't; don't
iken opinion
iki breath
iki (na) smart, stylish
iki(-) (infinitive of **iku** "going")
ikioi vigor, energy, spirit
ikimas', iku goes
ikiru (ikite imas') lives, is alive
ik-ko one (piece)
iku (ikimas') goes
ikura how much
ikutsu how many; how old
ima now
imas', iru is, stays

imi meaning
imo potato
imōto younger sister
in seal, stamp
inai within
inaka country
inchiki fake, fraud
Indo India
Indoneshiya Indonesia
ine rice-plant
infure inflation
inki ink
inki (na) gloomy
inochi one's life
inori prayer
inshō impression
interi intellectual ; highbrow
inu dog
ippai 1. full 2. a cupful (glassful)
...irai since ...
Irasshai(mase)! Welcome !
irasshaimas', irassharu (someone honored)
1. comes ; 2. goes ; 3. stays, is
ireba false teeth
iremas', ireru puts in, lets in
iriguchi entrance
irimas', iru[1] 1. is necessary ; needs ; wants
└2. roasts 3. shoots
iru[2] **(imas')** is, stays
iro color ; sex

isha doctor, physician
ishi[1] stone
ishi[2] will, intention
isogashii busy
isogimas', isogu hurries, rushes
issai all, everything, without exception
issaku-ban(-jitsu) night (day) before last
issho (ni) together with
isshō one's whole life
isshō-kemmei desperately; very hard
isshu a kind, a sort
isu chair
ita board, plank
itai painful, hurting
itami an ache, a pain
itashimas', itasu I (humbly) do
itazura mischief, prank
itchi agreement
ito thread, yarn; silk
itoko cousin
itoma =**hima**
itsu when
itsu-ka 1. 5 days; 5th day 2. sometime
itsutsu five
itsuwari falsehood, lie
ittai ...on earth, ...indeed
itte 1. going, goes and (gerund of **iku**) 2. =**yutte:** saying, says and (gerund of **yū**)
ittei fixed, settled, definite

ittō first, first class
iwa rock, crag
iwai celebration, party
iwayuru so-called, what you might call
iya no
iya (na) unpleasant; disagreeable; disliked
iyashii lowly, vulgar
iyo-iyo 1. at last 2. in fact 3. more and more
izen since, before, ago

J

ja, jā well, well then; in that case; now
ja arimasen (ja nai) it is not; it is not a case of
jagaimo Irish potatoes
jama interference, disturbance, hindrance, obstacle
jari gravel, pebbles
ji[1] a letter; a Chinese character
ji[2] hemorrhoids
ji[3] land, ground; texture; fabric
-ji o'clock
jibiki dictionary
jibun oneself; myself; alone
jidai age, period, era, time
jidōsha automobile
jidō-teki automatic
jigyō enterprise, business
jihen incident, happening
jijō circumstances; conditions

jikan time ; hour
jika ni directly ; personally
jiki ni immedately ; soon
jikken experiment
jikkō performance ; practice ; realization
jiko accident
jiku axis, axle
jiman pride, boast
jimi plain, sober
jimu business, office work
jimuin office clerk
jimusho office
-jin person
jinkō population
jisatsu suicide
jishin[1] earthquake
jishin[2] self-confidence
jissai actual conditions, reality ; in practice ; in fact, really
jitensha bicycle
jitsu truth ; truly, really
jitsugyō business
jitsugyō-ka businessman
jitsuyō practical use, utility
jiyū freedom, free ; fluent, at ease
jōbu healthy, sturdy
jochū maid-servant
jōdan joke
jokyū waitress
jōriku disembarking, landing

jorō(-ya) whore(-house)
jōsha getting into a car, boarding
... joshi Madame, Miss, Mrs.
jōshiki common sense
jōtai condition, situation, circumstances
jōtō the best, first-rate
jōzu skilled, clever, good at
jū[1] ten
jū[2] gun
-jū throughout the...
jūbako nestling boxes, Chinese boxes
jūbun enough
jūdō jujitsu
jū-hachi eighteen
jū-ichi eleven
jūji a cross
jūku nineteen
jukugo a compound word
jū-man a hundred thousand
jumbi preparations
jun order, turn
jun (na) pure
jū-ni twelve
jun-jimas', -jiru applies correspondingly; is made to accord with
junjo order
junkan circulation; cycle
junsa policeman
jū-roku sixteen
jūsho residence

jūsu 1. orange soda pop 2. juice
jūtan rug, carpet
jūyō important
juzu beads

K

ka mosquito
...ka ? QUESTION PARTICLE
...ka some ..., any ...
...ka... ... or ...
kabe wall
kabin flower vase
kabu stock (in a company)
kabushiki kaisha a corporation
kaburimas', kaburu wears on head
kachimas', katsu wins
kado (outside) corner
kaemas', kaeru[1] changes, exchanges
kaerimas', kaeru[2] goes home, goes back
kaeru[3] frog
kaeshimas', kaesu returns it
kaette contrary to expectations
kagaku science
kagami mirror
kage shade
kage-bōshi shadow
kagi key
kagimas', kagu smells it

kagiri limit, extent
kago basket
kagu furniture
kagu (kagimas') smells it
kai a meeting
-kai times, occasions
kaichū one's pocket
kaidan steps, stairs
kaidō an auditorium
kaigai overseas, abroad
kaigan seashore
kaigi meeting, conference
kaigun navy
kaii itchy
kaikan a public hall, a building
kaikei accounts
kaimas', kau[1] buys
kaimas', kau[2] raises, keeps (animals)
kaimono shopping
kaisha company
kaiwa conversation
kaji a fire
kajirimas', kajiru gnaws, nibbles
kakarimas', kakaru 1. it hangs 2. it takes, it requires 3. begins
kake 1. gambling; a bet 2. credit
kakemas', kakeru[1] 1. hangs it 2. telephones
kakemas', kakeru[2] bets
kakemas', kakeru[3] runs, gallops

kakemas', kakeru[4] multiplies
kaki[1] persimmon
kaki[2] oyster
kakimas', kaku writes; scratches
kakitome registered mail
kakomimas', kakomu surrounds
kaku writes; scratches
kakuremas', kakureru it hides
kakushimas', kakusu hides it
kama 1. pot; boiler 2. stove, oven, kiln 3. sickle
kamado kitchen range, stove
kamaimasen it makes no difference
kamban signboard
kami[1] hair (on the head)
kami[2] paper
kami-sama God; gods
kaminari thunder
kamisori razor
kamits'kimas', kamits'ku bites
kamo 1. wild duck 2. sucker, dupe
...ka mo shiremasen maybe ...
kampai a toast, "bottoms up"
kampan deck
kan a can
-kan for the interval of
kana Japanese syllabic writing
kanai my wife
kanamono hardware

kanarazu for sure
kanari fairly, rather
kanashii sad
kane money ; metal ; bell
kangae thought, idea, opinion
kangaemas', **kangaeru** thinks
kangofu nurse
kani crab
kanji[1] feeling
kanji[2] a Chinese character (letter)
kanjimas', **kanjiru** feels
kanjō bill
kankei connection, relationship, interest, concern
kan-kiri can opener
kankō sightseeing
kankōkyaku tourist
kanōsei possibility
kansha thanks, gratitude
kanshin[1] concern, interest
kanshin[2] **shimas'** admires
kanshō interference, meddling
kantan simple
kanzei customs duty
kanzen perfect
kanzō liver
kao face ; looks, a look
kapparaimas', **kapparau** swipes, steals, shoplifts
kara[1] shell, crust
kara[2] empty

...kara from ; since ; because, so
karada body
karai 1. spicy, hot, peppery 2. salty
karashi mustard
karasu crow
kare he, him
kare-ra they, them ⌈band
kare-shi lover, paramour ; boy friend ; hus-
karē curry
karē-raisu rice curry
kari temporary
karimas', kariru borrows
karimas', karu cuts, mows
karui light (of weight)
kasa umbrella
kasanarimas', kasanaru they pile up
kasanemas', kasaneru piles them up, puts one on top of another
kasegimas', kasegu earns, works for (money)
kashi (o-kashi) cakes, sweets, pastry
kashima rooms for rent
kashimas' kasu lends
...ka shira I wonder if...
kashiya house for rent
kasu sediment, dregs
kasu (kashimas') lends
kasumi haze, mist
kata[1] shoulder
kata[2] form, shape, size, mold, pattern

kata[3] person, honored person
-kata manner of doing, way
katachi form, shape
katagi respectable, steady, honest
katahō, kattappō one of a pair; the other one (of a pair)
katai hard; strong; upright; strict
katakana the squarish Japanese letters
katamari a lump
katamukimas', katamuku leans
katana sword
katarimas', kataru relates, tells
katawa cripple
katazukemas', katazukeru puts in order, straightens up, cleans up
katei[1] home, household, family
katei[2] hypothesis, supposition
katsu (kachimas') wins
katsu a Japanese "cutlet"; anything fried in deep fat
katsudō action, activity, movement, liveliness
katsugimas', katsugu carries on shoulders
katsuo (-bushi) a (dried) bonito fish
katsura a wig
katte[1] kitchen
katte[2] **(ni)** selfish(ly), as one wants to
kau[1] **(kaimas')** buys
kau[2] **(kaimas')** raises, keeps (animals)
kawa[1] river
kawa[2] skin

kawaii, kawairashii cute, loveable, darling
kawai-sō pitiful
kawakimas'. kawaku gets dry
kawara tile
kawari change , substitute
kawarimas' kawaru it changes; it takes the place of
kawase a money order
kaya mosquito net
kayōbi Tuesday
kayoimas'. kayou commutes, goes back and forth, goes (regularly)
kayu rice-gruel, porridge
kayui itchy
kazan volcano
kazari (-mono) ornament, decoration
kazarimas', kazaru decorates
kaze 1. wind 2. a cold
kazoemas', kazoeru counts
kazoku family
kazu number
ke hair, wool, feathers
kechim-bo stingy person, skinflint
kedo = keredo(mo)
kega wound, injury
keiba horse racing
keiba-jō a racetrack
keibetsu despise
keiei management, operation
keikaku plan, scheme

keiken experience
kieki business conditions, prosperity, boom
keiko exercise, practice, drill
keirin bicycle race
keisan calculation, computation
keisatsu police
keishiki form, formality
keiyaku contract, agreement
keizai economics, finances
kēki a cake
kekka result ; as a result (consequence)
kekkō 1. splendid ; excellent 2. fairly well, well enough ; enough
Kekkō des'. No, thank you.
kekkon marriage
kekkyoku after all, in the long run
kembutsu sightseeing
kempei MP ; shore patrol
kempō constitution
kemuri smoke
ken a Japanese prefecture (like a state)
kenchiku construction ; architecture
kencho the prefectural government (office)
kenka quarrel
kenkō health
kenkyū research, study
kensa, kensatsu inspection, examination, check-up
ken-yaku economy, thrift, economizing
ke-orimono woolen goods

keredo(mo) however, though, but
kerimas', keru kicks
keshiki scenery, view
keshimas', kesu puts out ; turns off ; erases
keshō cosmetics, make-up
keshō-shitsu ladies lounge
kessan settling accounts
kesseki absent
kesshin determination, resolution
kesu (keshimas') puts out ; turns off ; erases
kettei determination, decision
ketten flaw, defect
ki[1] spirit ; feeling ; mind, heart
ki[2] tree ; wood
kibishii strict, severe
kibō hope
kibun feeling, mood
kichi military base
ki-chigai mad, insane
kichin-to punctual; precise; neat
kido entrance gate, wicket
kiemas', kieru is extinguished, goes out; fades, vanishes
ki-iro yellow
ki-ito raw silk
kiji[1] article, news item
kiji[2] pheasant
kikai[1] chance, opportunity
kikai[2] machine, machinery
kikan engine ; instrument ; agency

kikasemas', kikaseru lets someone hear, tells, informs
kiken danger, peril
kiki-me ga arimas' is effective
kikimas', kiku listens, hears ; obeys ; asks ; is effective, works
kikō climate
kikoemas', kikoeru can be heard, can hear
kiku (**kikimas'**) listens, hears; obeys; asks; is effective, works
kiku chrysanthemum
kimarimas', kimaru is settled, is arranged
kimas'[1], **kuru** comes
kimas[2], **kiru** wears
kimben industrious, hardworking
kime grain, texture
kimemas', kimeru settles, arranges
kimi[1] you
kimi[2] feeling, sensation
kim-makie gold lacquer
kimo liver
kimochi feeling, sensation
kimono clothes ; a kimono
kimpatsu blond
kimyō strange, peculiar
kin gold
kina quinine
kinen commemoration
kinem-bi anniversary
Kin-en No Smoking
kingyo goldfish
kinjo neighborhood, vicinity

kinō yesterday
ki-no-doku pitiful, pitiable
kinoko mushrooms
kinshi prohibition, ban
kinu silk
kin-yōbi Friday
kin-yū finance
kinzoku metal
kioku memory
kippu ticket
kirai is disliked ; dislikes
kire a piece, a cut
kirei pretty ; clean
kiremas', kireru 1. cuts (well) 2. runs out 3. breaks down
kireme a gap, a break, a pause
kiri[1] fog, mist
kiri[2] a hole-punch, an awl, a drill
kiri[3] paulownia (tree or wood)
. . . (k)kiri only, just
kirimas', kiru cuts
kiritsu discipline
kiro 1. kilogram 2. kilometer 3. kilowatt 4. kiloliter
kiroku record
kiru[1] **(kirimas')** cuts
kiru[2] **(kimas')** puts on, wears
kiryō personal appearance, looks ; ability
kisen steamship
kisetsu season
kisha[1] railroad train

kisha[2] newspaperman, reporter
kishi shore, coast, bank
kishukusha dormitory, boarding house
kisoku rule, regulation
kissa-ten a tearoom
kita[1] north
kita[2] came (past tense of **kuru**) ; wore (past tense of **kiru**)
kitanai dirty
kite coming, comes and (gerund of **kuru**); wearing, wears and (gerund of **kiru**)
kitsui 1. tight 2. severe 3. bold
kitsune fox
kitte stamp
kitto no doubt, surely
kiwa brink, edge
kiwadoi dangerous, delicate, ticklish
kiwamarimas', kiwamaru comes to an end ; gets carried to extremes
kiwamemas', kiwameru carries to extremes ; investigates thoroughly
kiwamete extremely
kizamimas', kizamu chops fine ; carves ; notches, nicks
kizashi symptoms, signs, indications
kizu wound ; crack, flaw ; fault, defect
kizu-ato scar
ko child ; person
kō[1] this way, so, like this
kō[2] incense
kōba factory

kobamimas', kobamu refuses, rejects ; opposes, resists
kōban police box
koboshimas', kobosu spills
kobu bump, knob, swelling
kobun henchman, subordinate, follower
kobune small boat
kobushi fist
kōcha black tea
kochira 1. here, this way 2. this one 3. me, I; us, we
kodai ancient times
kōdō[1] highway
kōdō[2] action, behavior
kodomo child ; boy
koe voice ; cry
kōen[1] public park
kōen[2] lecture
kōen[3] support
kōfu workman
kōfuku happiness
kōfun excitement
kōgai suburbs
kogashimas', kogasu scorches
kogata small-size (model)
kōgeki attack
kōgi lecture
kogimas', kogu rows
kogitte check
kōgo spoken language, colloquial
Kōgō sama the Empress

kogoe low voice, whisper
kogoto scolding
kogu (kogimas') rows
kōgyō industry
kōhei fair, impartial
kōhii coffee ; **-ten, -ya** coffeeshop
koi[1] carp (fish)
koi[2] love
koi[3] request
kōi goodwill
koibito sweetheart
koitsu this one
kōji construction work
kojiki beggar
kojin individual
kōjitsu excuse, pretext
kōkai public
kōkan exchange
koke moss
kōkishin curiosity, inquisitiveness
kokkai assembly, parliament, congress, Diet
kokkei amusing, funny
kokku cook
koko here, this place
kokonotsu nine
kokonoka 9 days ; the 9th day
kōkoku advertisement
kokoro mind, heart, spirit, feeling
kokoro-mochi feelings, spirit, mood

kokorozuke tip, gratuity
kokuban blackboard
kokubō national defense
Kokuden Government Electric (the Tokyo elevated)
Kokujin Negro
kokumin a people, a nation
kokunai internal, domestic, inland
kokuritsu national, government-run
kokusai international
kokuseki nationality
kokyō hometown, birthplace
kokyū respiration, breathing
koma a toy top
komakai 1. fine, small 2. detailed, exact 3. thrifty 4. small change
komarimas', komaru gets perplexed, embarrassed, is at a loss
komban tonight
Komban wa. Good evening.
kombō club, billy-club, bludgeon
kombu (kind of seaweed)
kome rice
komi-itta complicated, intricate, elaborate
komori babysitter
kōmori 1. bat 2. umbrella
kompon foundation, basis
kōmurimas', kōmuru sustains, suffers, incurs
kon dark blue
kona powder ; flour
kona-gusuri powdered medicine

konashimas', konasu powders ; digests
kondo this time ; next time
kongetsu this month
kongo from now on, in the future
konkūru prize contest
konna such a
konnan difficulty, trouble, hardship
Konnichi wa. Good afternoon. (Hello.)
kono this
kono-aida lately
konomimas', konomu likes, is fond of, prefers
kon-yaku engagement (to be married)
konzatsu confusion, jumble, disorder
koppu a glass, a cup
koraemas', koraeru 1. stands, bears 2. controls, restrains, represses
kore this one
kore-ra these
kōri[1] ice
kōri[2] baggage
kōritsu public, municipal
korogarimas', korogaru rolls, tumbles
koroshimas', korosu kills
koruku(-nuki) cork(-screw)
kōryo consideration, reflection
kōsa-ten an intersection (of streets)
kōsai social relations, company
koshi hips
koshi-kakemas', -kakeru sits down
koshimaki loincloth ; petticoat

koshimas', kosu goes over; exceeds
koshiraemas', koshiraeru makes, builds
koshō[1] 1. damage, something wrong 2. hindrance, impediment
koshō[2] pepper
kōshō negotiations; connections
kōshū the public, the masses
... koso indeed (it is ...)
kosu (koshimas') goes over; exceeds
kōsui perfume
kosurimas', kosuru rub, scrape
kotaemas', kotaeru answers
Kōtaishi sama the Crown Prince
kotchi = kochira
koto thing, matter; fact; case; experience
  ... (suru) koto ga aru does do it; does it sometimes; **... (suru) koto ga nai** never does it; **... (sh'ta) koto ga aru** has done it; **... (sh'ta) koto ga nai** has never done it
kotoba 1. word, words; sentence (spoken) 2. speech 3. language
kotonarimas', kotonaru is different, differs
koto-ni especially; moreover, what is more
kotoshi this year
kotowarimas', kotowaru 1. refuses, declines, begs off 2. makes excuses
kotowaza a proverb
kotozuke, kotozute a message (for someone)
kōtsū communication; traffic

kottō-hin curios, antiques
kowai 1. afraid ; frightful 2. terrific, swell
kowaremas', kowareru it breaks
kowashimas', kowasu breaks it
koya hut, shed
koyama hill
koyōji toothpick
kō yū this sort of, such
kōzan a mine
kozara saucer
kōzen open(ly), public(ly)
kozuchi a small hammer
kozukai[1] janitor ; attendant ; servant
kozukai[2] pin money, pocket money
kozutsumi package, parcel
ku[1] nine
ku[2] a ward (in a city)
kubarimas', kubaru distributes, allots ; deals (cards)
kubetsu difference ; discrimination
kubi neck
kubomi hollow, dent, depression
kuchi 1. mouth 2. words, speech 3. entrance ; hole, opening 4. cork, stopper 5. job opening
kuchi-beni lipstick
kuchimas', kuchiru rots, decays
kuda pipe, tube
kudakemas', kudakeru it breaks, it smashes
kudakimas', kudaku breaks it, smashes it
kudamono fruit

kudari down, going down ; descent
kudarimas', kudaru comes (goes) down ;
. . . kudasai please ⌊falls, drops
kudasaimas', kudasaru gives ; does the favor of
kudashi a purgative, a laxitive ; a vermıfuge
kudoi 1. long-winded, dull 2. thick, greasy
kufū device, scheme
kugatsu September
kugi nail
kugiri punctuation
kūgun air force
kui post, stake, pile
kuimas, kuu eats
kuji a lot (in a lottery)
kujira whale
kuki stalk, stem
kūki air
kuma bear
kumi a set, suit, pack ; a class, band, com-
kumiai association, guild, union ⌊pany
kumiawase assortment, mixture
kumimas' kumu ladles, scoops up ; considers, sympathize
kumitate structure, set-up, organization,
kumo[1] cloud ⌊frame-work
kumo[2] spider
kumorimas', kumoru gets cloudy
. . . kun young Mr. ...

kuni 1. country 2. native place, home area
kura[1] saddle
kura[2] warehouse, storeroom, cellar
kurabemas', kuraberu compares, contrasts
kurabu club
kurai[1] dark, gloomy
kurai[2] 1. grade, rank 2. situation; fix; as much as; to the extent; about, approximately
kurashimas', kurasu lives, gets by, makes a living
kurasu class
kuremas', kureru[1] gives; does the favor of
kuremas', kureru[2] gets dark
kuri chestnut
kuriimu cream
kuriiningu cleaning
kurimas', kuru winds, reels
Kurisumasu Christmas
kurō difficulties, hardships
kuroi black
kurōto expert, professional
kuru[1] **(kimas')** comes
kuru[2] **(kurimas')** winds, reels
kuruimas', kuruu goes mad, insane; gets warped; gets out of order
kuruma car; taxi; vehicle
kurushii painful; hard, heavy
kusa, k'sa grass, weed
kusai, k'sai smelly, stinking; fishy, questionable

kusari, k'sari chain
kusarimas', kusaru goes bad, rots, decays
kuse, k'se a habit
kushami, k'shami a sneeze
kushi 1. a comb 2. a skewer, a spit
kuso, k'so dung, excrement
kusugurimas', kusuguru tickles
kusuguttai ticklish
kusuri, k'suri medicine
kusuri-ya, k'suri-ya drugstore
kutabiremas', kutabireru gets tired
kutsu shoes
kutsu-bera shoehorn
kutsu-himo shoelace
kutsu-migaki shoeshine
kutsu-naoshi shoe-repairman
kutsu-shita, kutsu-sh'ta socks
kuttsukimas', kuttsuku sticks to
kuu (kuimas') eats ; bites
kuwa[1] hoe
kuwa[2] mulberry
kuwaemas', kuwaeru adds ; imposes
kuwashii detailed
kuzu waste, trash, rags
kuzushimas', kuzusu 1. cashes, changes, breaks (into small money) 2. breaks down, demolishes 3. simplifies
kyabarē cabaret, nightclub
kyabetsu cabbage

kyaku (o-kyaku) visitor, guest, customer
kyandē candy
kyarameru caramels
kyatsu = koitsu
kyō today
kyōdai brothers and sisters ; brother ; sister
kyōdō union, cooperation, joint
kyōgi[1] game, match, contest
kyōgi[2] conference, discussion
kyōiku education
kyōju professor
kyōkai church
kyoku office, bureau
kyokuba circus
kyokutō Far East
kyōmi interest
kyonen last year
kyori distance
Kyōsan-shugi (-shugisha) Communism, (-ist)
kyōshi teacher, instructor, tutor
kyōshitsu classroom, schoolroom
kyōsō competition, rivalry, contest
kyōtsū common, general
kyōyō[1] for common use, for public use
kyōyō[2] culture, education, refinement
kyū class, grade
kyūji waiter, waitress, steward, office-boy
kyūkō express (train, etc)
kyūri cucumber

kyūyo compensation, allowance, grant

M

ma room ; space ; time ; leisure
mā well ; I should say ; perhaps
machi town
machigai mistake
machimas', matsu waits for
mada (not) yet ; still
madara spots, spotted, polka dots
. . . made until ; as far as ; to
mado window
mae front ; in front of ; before
magarimas', magaru 1. turns, goes around 2. it bends, curves
magemas', mageru bends it, curves it
mago grandchild
mahi paralysis
mai- each
maiasa every morning
maiban every night
maido every time
maigo lost ; a lost child
mainen every year
mainichi every day ; all the time
mairimas', mairu 1. I come, I go 2. visits, calls on 3. is defeated, loses (a game, etc.) 4. is floored, stumped
maisō burial

Maitta ! You've got me !
majime serious, sober
majirimas', majiru mixes
majiwarimas', majiwaru associates with
makasemas', makaseru entrust with, leaves in one's hands
makashimas', makasu 1. beats down the price 2. defeats
makemas', makeru 1. comes down on the price 2. loses, is defeated 3. is inferior
maki[1] firewood
maki[2] a roll ; a volume
maki-e raised lacquer
makimas', maku rolls up ; winds ; wraps
makoto sincere ; faithful ; true ; genuine
makura pillow
. . . mama as it is ; as one wants
mame[1] beans
mame[2] blister, corn, bunion
mamorimas', mamoru defends, protects
man 10,000
man- fully
mane imitation
manekimas', maneku invites
manga cartoon, comics
man-ichi if by any chance
man-in full (of people)
mannaka the very middle
mannenhitsu fountain pen
Manshū Manchuria

manukaremas', manukareru escape from, be exempt from
manzai cross-talk comedy
mare rare
mari ball
maru circle, ring ; zero
maru- fully
maru de perfectly, completely
marui round
masarimas', masaru surpasses, is superior
machimas', matsu waits for
massaka-sama head over heels
massugu straight
masu (mashimas') increases, raises, swells
mata[1] again ; moreover
mata[2] groin ; crotch
mata-wa or, or else ; also
matchi match
mato aim, target
matomarimas', matomaru is settled, arranged, finished
matomemas', matomeru settles, arranges
matsu[1] pine tree
matsu[2] **(machimas')** waits for
matsuri a festival
mattaku quite, completely
mawarimas', mawaru goes around
mawashimas', mawasu turns around, passes around
mayoimas', mayou gets lost ; gets dazed ; gets perplexed

mayu 1. eyebrows 2. cocoon
mazu first of all, before anything else
mazui 1. untasty 2. awkward, poor 3. in-
mazushii poor, needy ⌊advisable 4. ugly
me 1. eye 2. bud
-me -th (**itsutu-me** "5th") ⌈order
mechamecha in pieces, all confused, in dis-
medetai 1. auspicious, happy 2. simple-
megane eyeglasses ⌊minded
mei niece ⌈tion, a famous product
meibutsu a local speciality, a special attrac-
meijin expert
meirei order, command
meishi calling card
meishi-ire calling card case
meiwaku trouble, annoyance
meiyo prestige, honor, glory
mekata weight
mekura blind
men[1] mask ; surface ; front
men[2] cotton
mendō trouble, difficulty, nuisance
menkai interview, meeting
meriyasu knitted goods
meshi cooked rice ; a meal ⌈drinks
meshiagarimas', meshiagaru 1. eats 2.
meshimas', mesu in formal speech can re-
place such verbs as *kimas'* (wears), *tabe-mas'* (eats), *nomimas'* (drinks), etc.

meshitsukai servant
me-tsuki a look (in one's eyes)
metta reckless, rash
metta ni+NEGATIVE VERB seldom
mezamashi (**-dokei**) alarm clock
mezurashii rare, uncommon, novel, curious
mi 1. fruit, nut 2. body
mi(**-**) INFINITIVE OF *miru* (seeing)
mibun social standing
miburi gesture, movement
michi street, road
michimas', michiru is complete, is full
midare disorder
midashimas', midasu throws into disorder
midori green
miemas', mieru 1. is visible, can be seen 2. shows up, comes
migakimas', migaku polishes, shines
migi right
migoto splendid, beautiful
migurushii unseemly, unsightly
mihon a sample
mijikai short (not long)
mikan tangerine
mikata 1. a friend, an accomplice 2. a view-point 3. opinion
mikka 3 days; 3rd day
mikomi 1. promise, hope 2. expectation
mimai a visit (especially of sympathy, etc.)
mimas', miru sees, looks; tries doing
mimi ear

mimi-wa earring
mina-san you all, everybody
minami south
mine peak, summit
minkan the people ; civilians ; civil
mino straw raincoat
minori crop, harvest
minshu-shugi democracy
minshū the masses, the people
min-yō folk song, ballad
minzoku race
mirin sweet saké
miru (mimas') sees, looks ; tries doing
miruku milk
mise store, shop
misemas', miseru shows
misemono exhibition, exhibit
mishin sewing machine
miso bean paste
misu bamboo blind
mitashimas', mitasu fills up, satisfies
mitomemas', mitomeru recognizes, admits
mitsukarimas', mitsukaru is found, discovered
mitsukemas', mitsukeru finds, discovers
mittsu three
miukemas', miukeru observes, happens to see
miya a Shinto shrine
miyage a present, a souvenir

miyako capital, city
mizo drain, ditch
mizu (cold) water
mizuumi a lake
...mo also, too
...mo ...mo both...and...; neither... nor...
mō 1. already; now 2. more
mochi rice cake
mochimas', motsu has, holds, carries
mochiron of course
modoshimas', modosu 1. vomits 2. sends back, returns
mohan model, pattern
moji letter, character, writing
mōkemas', mōkeru[1] makes money, profits
mōkemas', mōkeru[2] prepares, sets up
Mōko Mongolia
mokuhan woodblock print
mokuhyō target, goal
mokuroku catalog, list, table, inventory
mokutan charcoal
mokuteki aim, objective, purpose
mokuyōbi Thursday
mokuyoku bathing
momen cotton
momiji 1. maples 2. autumn leaves
momimas', momu massages; rubs; pounds on
momo 1. peach 2. hip, thigh
mon[1] family crest
mon[2] gate

mondai question, problem, topic
mon(o) 1. thing 2. person
...(sh'ta) mon(o) des' used to...
...mono because
mono- (emphatic prefix with adjectives)
monogatari a tale, a legend
monozuki curious, inquisitive
moppara principally, chiefly
moraimas', morau receives, gets ; has some one do for one
morashimas', morasu lets leak ; reveals
moremas', moreru leaks out ; is omitted
mori woods, forest
morimas', moru piles it up, accumulates it
moroi brittle, frail
mōru lace
moshi if
moshi moshi! hello! hey! say!
mōshikomi application
mōshimas', mōsu 1. I say 2. I do
moto 1. origin, source 2. (at the) foot (of)
motomemas', motomeru 1. wants, looks for 2. asks for 3. buys, gets
moto-yori from the beginning ; by nature
motozukimas', motozuku is based on ; conforms to
motsu (mochimas') has, holds, carries
mottai-nai 1. is undeserving 2. it is wasteful
motte ikimas' (iku) takes

motte imas' (iru) has, holds
motte kimas' (kuru) brings
motto more, still more; longer
motto-mo 1. most, exceedingly 2. indeed, of course 3. but, however
moyō pattern
mucha unreasonable ; reckless ; disorderly
muchi a whip
muchū trance, ecstasy
muda futile, no good, wasteful ; useless
mudan de without notice, without permission
mugi grain ; wheat, barley
mugiwara straw
mugoi cruel, brutal
muika 6 days ; the 6th day
mujaki naive, innocent, unsophisticated
mujō heartless
mujun inconsistent; contradiction
mukaemas', mukaeru meets ; welcomes ; invites
mukaimas', mukau opposes ; heads for
mukashi ancient times
mukimas', muku 1. faces 2. skins, pares
muko son-in-law ; bridegroom
mukō opposite, across the way ; over there (in America, etc.)
mukuimas', mukuiru repays ; compensates
mumei nameless, anonymous
munashii empty ; futile, in vain
mune[1] chest, breast ; heart, mind
mune[2] purport, effect, intent

mura village
mure group, throng, flock
muri (shimas') (is) unreasonable, violent; overdoes; asking too much
muryō free of charge
mushi insect; worm
mushi-atsui muggy, close, sultry, humid
mushi-ba decayed tooth
mushi-kudashi vermifuge, worm remedy
mushimas', musu steams; is sultry, humid
musubimas', musubu ties; ties up, winds up; wears a tie
musuko, mus'ko son
musume daughter; girl
muttsu six
muyō unnecessary; useless; having no business
muzukashii hard, difficult
muzumuzu itchy, crawly, creepy
myō strange, queer
myōgonichi day after tomorrow
myōnichi tomorrow

N

n'=no
na[1] name
na[2] greens, vegetables
. . . na! isn't it, don't-you-know, you see
nabe pan, pot
nademas' naderu soothes, pets

nae seedling
nagai, nagaku long
. . . -nagara while ...-ing
nagaremas', nagareru flows
nagashi kitchen sink
nagashimas', nagasu lets flow
nagaya tenement house
nagekimas', nageku weeps, moans, laments
nagemas', nageru throws
nagurimas', naguru knock, beat, strike
nagusame comfort, consolation
nagusami amusement, entertainment
nai (arimasen) there is no..., has no ..., lacks
naichi inside the country, inland, internal
naifu knife
naigai inside and out ; home and abroad ; approximately
naikaku a government cabinet
naka 1. inside, in 2. relations, terms (between people)
nakama friend, pal
nakanaka extremely (long, hard, bad, etc.), more than one might expect
...-nakereba unless
...-nakereba narimasen must, has to
nakimas', naku weeps ; cries ; makes an animal sound
naku(te) without
nama 1. raw, uncooked; fresh 2. hard cash
namae name
namaiki impertinent
namakemas', namakeru idles, is lazy

namari 1. lead (metal) 2. dialect, accent
Nambei South America
namboku north and south
nambu the south, the southern part
namemas', nameru licks, tastes
nami[1] ordinary, common, average
nami[2] wave
namida tear
nana(tsu) seven
naname slanting, oblique, at an angle, diagonal
nan(i) what
nan-, nam- how many...
nan dai=nan des' ka what is it
nan de mo anything at all
nanibun anyway, anyhow
nan-nara if you prefer, if you like; if you don't want to
nan no what (kind of); of what
nanoka 7 days; the 7th day
nao still more; moreover
naorimas', naoru is corrected, repaired, cured, fixed
naoshimas', naosu corrects, repairs, cures, fixes
...nara if
narabemas', naraberu arranges, lines them up
narabimas', narabu they line up, arrange themselves
naraimas', narau learns
narashimas', narasu 1. smoothes, averages 2. domesticates, tames 3. sounds, rings it
naremas', nareru gets used to, grows

familiar with
nari form ; personal appearance
narimas', naru[1] becomes, gets to be, turns into ; is completed ; is, amounts to
narimas', naru[2] (fruit) is borne
narimas', naru[3] it sounds, rings
naru-hodo I see ; quite so ; you are so right
nasake affection, feeling, tenderness, compassion
nashi pear
. . . -nashi without
nashimas', nasu achieves, forms, does
nasu eggplant
nata hatchet
natsu summer
natsu-mikan Japanese grapefruit
nawa rope, cord
naya barn, shed
nayami suffering, distress, torment
naze why
nazo riddle
ne 1. root 2. sound 3. sleeping 4. price
. . . ne ! (nē !) isn't it, don't-you-know, you see
nebari stickiness
negaimas', negau asks for, requests, begs
neji screw
neji-mawashi screwdriver
neko cat
nekutai necktie
nemas', neru goes to bed, lies down, sleeps

nemmatsu the end of the year
nemui sleepy
nemurimas', nemuru sleeps
nen[1] year
nen[2] deliberation, attention
nenryō fuel
neraimas', nerau aims at, watches for, seeks
neru[1] **(nemas')** goes to bed, lies down, sleeps
neru[2] **(nerimas')** kneads
neru flannel
nē-san big sister ; Miss ; Waitress !
netsu fever ; heat
neuchi value, worth
nezumi mouse, rat
ni[1] two
ni[2] load, burden
. . . ni in, at ; to ; for ; with ; and
niaimas', niau is becoming, suits
nibui dull
Nichi- Japanese
nichiyōbi Sunday
ni-do two times
niemas', nieru it boils, it cooks
nigashimas', nigasu turns loose ; lets get away
nigemas', nigeru runs away, escapes
nigirimas', nigiru grasps, grips, clutches
nigiyaka merry, bustling, lively, flourishing
Nihon Japan
Nihon-jin a Japanese

Nihongo Japanese (language)
Nihon-sei made in Japan
nii-san big brother
niji rainbow
ni-jū 1. twenty 2. double, duplicate
nikai 1. second floor, upstairs 2. two times
nikibi pimple
nikoniko smiling
niku meat
nikui dislikable, hated; hard, difficult
nikutai flesh, the body
nikuya butcher
nimas'[1], **niru** resembles
nimas'[2], **niru** boils, cooks
nimotsu baggage, load
nimpu coolie, workman
-nin person
ninaimas', ninau carries on shoulders
ningen human being
ningyō doll
ninjō human nature, human feelings, warm-heartedness
ninki popularity
ninsoku coolie, workman
ninshin pregnancy
ninshin-chūzetsu abortion
nioi a smell
nira a leek; a green onion
niramimas', niramu glares, stares
niru[1] (**nimas'**) boils, cooks

niru[2] (**nimas'**) resembles
nise phony, imitation
nishiki brocade
nishin herring
nisu varnish
ni-tō 2nd class
niwa garden
niwatori chicken
no (**no-hara**) field
...no 1. SUBORDINATING PARTICLE: of, pertaining to, in, at 2. = **da** which is 3. the one 4. (= **koto**) the fact, the act
nobashimas', nobasu; nobemas', noberu[1] extends it, reaches; spreads it
nobemas', noberu[2] tells, relates
nobimas', nobiru it extends, reaches; it spreads
noborimas', noboru climbs, goes up
nodo throat
nodo ga kawakimash'ta is thirsty
nōgyō agriculture
no-hara field
nokemas', nokeru removes; omits
noki eaves
nokogiri a saw
nokorimas', nokoru remains, is left behind (over)
nokoshimas', nokosu leaves behind (over)
nokimas', noku gets out of the way
nomi[1] chisel
nomi[2] flea

nomimizu drinking water
nomimono beverage, something to drink
nōmin the farmers
nomimas', nomu drinks
nonki easygoing, happy-go-lucky
noren shop curtain ; credit
nori 1. paste ; starch 2. seaweed
norikaemas', norikaeru changes (trains, buses, etc.)
norimas', noru gets aboard, rides
nōritsu efficiency
noroi slow, dull
noru (norimas') gets aboard, rides ; is found in
nosemas', noseru loads, puts aboard, ships ; publishes
nōzei payment of taxes
. . . nozoite except for, with the exception of
nozokimas', nozoku 1. peeps at 2. removes, eliminates ; omits
nozomashii desirable, welcome
nozomimas', nozomu desires, looks to, hopes for; looks out on
nugimas', nugu takes off (clothes, shoes, etc.)
nuguimas', nuguu wipes away
nuimas', nuu sews
nukemas', nukeru comes off ; escapes ; is omitted
nukimas', nuku uncorks ; removes ; omits ; surpasses ; selects
numa swamp, marsh
nurashimas', nurasu wets, dampens
nuremas', nureru gets wet, damp

nuri lacquer, varnish, painting
nurimono lacquerware
nurimas', nuru lacquers, paints, varnishes
nurui lukewarm ; sluggish
nushi master, owner
nusumimas', nusumu steals, swipes, robs
nuu (**nuimas'**) sews
nyūbai the rainy season
nyūgaku admission to a school, entering a school
nyūin entering a hospital, hospital admission
nyūjō-ken admission ticket
nyūsu news
nyūyō necessary, needed
nyūyoku bath, taking a bath

O

o[1] (**=shippo**) tail
o[2] thong, strap (**=hanao**)
... o DIRECT OBJECT PARTICLE
o- HONORIFIC PREFIX: "your" or "that common thing we often talk about"
ō- big, great
oba(**san**) aunt ; lady
obā(**san**) grandmother ; old lady
obi belt, sash
oboemas', oboeru remembers
obuimas', obuu carries on one's back
o-cha Japanese green tea

ochimas', ochiru falls; drops; is omitted; fails; runs away; is inferior [cool
ochitsukimas', ochitsuku calms down, keeps
ōdan[1] jaundice
ōdan[2] crossing, going across, intersecting
odorimas', odoru dances
odorokimas', odoroku is surprised, aston-
oemas', oeru finishes, completes [ished
ōfuku round trip [respect
ogamimas', ogamu worships; looks at with
ōgata large-size (model)
ōgesa exaggerated
ogi a reed
ōgi a folding fan
oginaimas', oginau completes; complements; makes good, makes up for
ōgoe de in a loud voice [person to
ogorimas', ogoru is extravagant; treats a
o-hachi a rice bucket
ohako hobby; specialty, trick
Ohayō (gozaimas')! Good morning!
o-hiya cold water
oi nephew
oi! hey!
ōi, ōku many, numerous [stays
oide (ni narimas') 1. comes 2. goes 3. is,
oimas', ou[1] chases, pursues
oimas', ou[2] carries on back
ōimas', ōu covers, shields

oiru (lubricating) oil (*for car*)
oishii tasty, nice, delicious
oji (**san**) uncle
o-jigi a polite bow
ojii-san grandfather
ojoku disgrace, shame, scandal
ojō-san a young lady; your daughter
oka hill; dry land
okabu=**ohako**
okage sama de thanks to your kind attitude; thank you (I'm very well *or* it's going very nicely).
okame moonfaced woman
okami landlady, woman
ōkami wolf
o-kane money
okāsan mother
okashii amusing, funny
okashimas', okasu commits, perpetrates; violates, encroaches upon
ōkata 1. for the most part 2. probably
o-kawari 1. a second helping 2. change (in health)
okazu side dishes (*anything but rice*)
oke tub, wooden bucket
oki offshore
...-oki ni at intervals of ...
okiba a place (to put something)
ōkii, ōki na big, large

okimas',[1] **oku** puts ; does for later
okimas',[2] **okiru** gets up
okimono an ornament ; bric-a-brac
o-kome rice
okonaimas', okonau acts, does, carries out, performs ⌈from
okorimas', okoru[1] 1. happens 2. springs
okorimas', okoru[2] gets mad (angry)
okoshimas', okosu raises ; establishes ; gets a person up
okotarimas', okotaru neglects; is lazy about
ok'-san wife
oku[1] a hundred million
oku[2] the back or inside part
oku[3] **(okimas')** puts ; does for later
ōku lots ; mostly
okubi belch ⌈runs slow
okuremas', okureru is late ; falls behind ;
okurimono gift, present
okurimas', okuru 1. presents, awards with 2. sends ; sees a person off ; spends (time)
omake extra, bonus, premium; to boot
omaru bed-pan ; chamberpot
omawari-san policeman ⌈on back
ombu (shimas') carries baby on back ; rides
omedetō (gozaimas') congratulations; happy new year ⌈3. invites
omeshi (ni narimas') 1. wears 2. buys
omocha toy

omoi heavy; important
omoi-dashimas', -dasu remembers, recollects
omoimas', omou thinks, feels
omo na principal, main
omoshiroi interesting, pleasant, amusing, fun
omou thinks, feels
ōmu a parrot
omuretsu omelet
omutsu diapers
on[1] obligation; kindness
on[2] sound; pronunciation
onaji same
onaka stomach
onaka ga s'kimash'ta is hungry
onara flatulence, wind
ondo temperature
ongaku music
oni devil, ogre
onna woman, female
ono ax, hatchet
onore self
onozukara automatically, spontaneously
onsen hot spring
ōrai[1] traffic; communication; thoroughfare
ōrai[2] "all right" (all clear, go ahead)
Oranda Holland, Dutch
orenji orange, orange drink
oremas' oreru it breaks; it folds
ori[1] time, occasion

ori[2] cage ; jail
orime fold, crease, pleat
orimono textiles, cloth
orimas', oriru gets down, gets off
orimas', oru[1] is, stays = (**imas', iru**)
orimas', oru[2] breaks (folds, bends) it
orimas', oru[3] weaves
oroshimas', orosu takes down ; unloads ; invests ; drops (from a car), lets out (of vehicle)
osaemas', osaeru represses, restrains, controls
o-sake = **sake**[1]
osamemas', osameru 1. reaps, harvests ; gets 2. pays ; finishes 3. governs ; pacifies
oseji compliment, flattery
oshaberi chatterbox, gossip
oshare dandy, fancy dresser
oshiemas', oshieru teaches, shows, tells, informs
oshii 1. regrettable 2. precious
oshiire closet, cupboard
oshimas', osu pushes
oshiroi face powder
Ōshū, Europe
osoi late ; slow
osoreirimas' 1. excuse me 2. thank you
osoremas', osoreru fears
osoroshii fearful, dreadful
osshaimas', ossharu (someone honored) says ; is called

osu (**oshimas'**) pushes
Ōs'torariya Australia
oto sound, noise
otoko man, male, boy
otona adult
otonashii gentle, well-behaved
otori decoy ; lure
otoroemas', otoroeru declines, fades, grows weak
otorimas', otoru is inferior, worse
otoshimas', otosu drops
otōto younger brother
ototoi day before yesterday
ototoshi year before last
otsu chic, stylish
ou (**oimas'**)[1] chases, pursues
ou (**oimas'**)[2] carries on back
ōu (**ōimas'**) covers, shields
owarimas', owaru it ends
oya parent
oya-bun boss, ringleader, chief
ōyake public, open, official
oyatsu snack (esp. mid-afternoon)
ōyō application, putting to use
oyobi and also
oyobimas', oyobu reaches, extends to, equals
oyogimas', oyogu swims
ō-yorokobi de with great delight
oyoso about, roughly
ōzei large crowd, throng

P

pa . . . ! all gone ; boom!
pachinko pinball
pāma permanent wave
pan bread
panku puncture, blowout
pan-s'ke pompom girl
pan-ya bakeshop
paripari crisp ; first-rate
pēji page
penki paint
pikapika flashing, glittering
pinto focus
poketto pocket
pomādo pomade, hair oil
pombiki a pimp, a hustler
posuto, pos'to a mailbox
potsu a dot
puro-resu professional wrestling
pūru 1. swimming pool 2. motor pool, parking lot

R

-ra and others ; all of
raigetsu next month
raikyaku guest, caller, visitor
rainen next year

raishū next week
rajio radio
raku ease, comfort, comfortable
rakudai failure (in a test)
rakugaki scribbling; doodling
rambō violence, outrage; disorderly
rāmen Chinese noodles
ramma transom window (opening)
ramune lemonade
ran 1. orchid 2. column
ranchi 1. lunch 2. launch
randoseru knapsack
rappa trumpet
. . . rashii probably; it seems like; it looks like
rebā 1. liver 2. lever
rei[1] **(o-rei)** greeting; thanks
rei[2] **(maru)** zero
rei[3] precedent, example
reibō (-sōchi) air conditioning
reigai exception (to the rule)
reigi courtesy
reizōko refrigerator, icebox
rekishi history
rekōdo record
remon lemon
ren-ai love
renchū gang, crowd, clique
renga brick
rengō union, alliance, Allied

renraku connection; relevancy
renshū training, practice, drill
ressha a train
retsu row, line
rettō archipelago, chain of islands
ri advantage, profit, interest
rieki benefit, advantage, profit
rihatsu-ten barbershop
rikai understanding, comprehension
rikō clever, sharp
riku land
rikugun army
rikutsu reason, logic, argument
rin a bell, a doorbell
ringo apple
rinji extraordinary, special, emergency
rinki emergency; expedient
rippa fine, splendid; well
rireki personal history, summary of one's career
rishi interest
risō ideal
risu squirrel
ritsu 1. rate, proportion 2. a cut, a percentage
rittai solid; 3-D, stereoscopic
riyō use, utilization
riyū reason
rōdō-sha worker, laborer
roji alley
rōka passage, corridor, aisle

roku six
Rōma Rome
rōma-ji romanization, Latin letters
ron argument, discussion ; treatise
rōnin an unemployed samurai ; a boy between schools ; a man without a job
ronri logic
Roshiya Russia
rōsoku candle
rōsu-biifu roastbeef
rōzu waste, refuse; damaged goods
rumpen tramp, hobo
rusu 1. absent, away from home 2. taking care of the house while one is away
rusu-ban someone to take care of the house in one's absence
ryakushimas', ryakusu abbreviates, shortens ; omits
ryō 1. hunting ; fishing (as sport) 2. dormitory, boardinghouse 3. mound, mausoleum 4. territory 5. quantity.
ryōgae money exchange
ryōhō both
ryōji (-kan) consul(ate)
ryokan inn
ryoken passport
ryokō travel, trip
ryokyaku traveler, passenger
ryōri cooking
ryōri-ten, -ya a restaurant

ryōshin[1] both parents
ryōshin[2] conscience
ryūkō popularity, vogue
Ryūkyū the Ryukyus (Okinawa, etc.)

S

sā well ; come on
... sa ! EMPHATIC PARTICLE
sabi rust
sabishii lonely
sābisu service ; free (as part of the service)
saborimas', saboru cuts class; plays hookey
sadamarimas', sadamaru is settled, fixed
sadamemas', sadameru settles it, fixes it
... sae even ; only
sagarimas', sagaru it hangs down ; goes down
sagashimas', sagasu looks for
sagemas', sageru 1. lets it hang down ; lowers 2. carries (hanging)
sagurimas', saguru gropes
sai[1] talent, ability
sai[2] side-dish
sai[3] time, occasion
sai[4] wife
saiban trial, court decision
saichū midst
saifu purse
saigo last, final

saijō best, highest
saiku work(manship), ware
saishin newest, up-to-date
saisho the very beginning (first)
saishū final, the very end (last)
saiwai good fortune
saji spoon
saka hill, slope
sakan flourishing, prosperous; splendid, vigorous
sakana 1. fish 2. appetizers with liquor
sakasama upside down
sakazuki wine cup, saké cup
sake[1] saké (Japanese rice-wine)
sake[2] salmon
sakebimas', sakebu cries out, shouts
sakemas', sakeru avoids
saki 1. front; future; ahead 2. point, tip
saki-hodo a little while ago
sakimas', saku blooms, blossoms
sakku condom
sakura cherry tree
sakurambo a cherry
sam- = **san-**
...sama = **...san** Mr., Mrs., Miss
samatagemas', samatageru obstructs, hinders
samayoimas', samayou wanders about
sama-zama diverse, all kinds
samemas', sameru[1] wakes up, comes to one's senses

samemas', sameru[2] gets cold, cools off
sampo a walk
samui cold, chilly
san three
-san 1. Mr., Mrs., Miss 2. mountain
sangyō industry
sanka participation
sankaku triangle
sansei approval, support
santō third class
sao pole, rod
sappari 1. not at all 2. clean; fresh 3. frank
sara plate, dish ; saucer ; ashtray
sarada salad
saru monkey
sasemas', saseru makes (do), lets (do), has (do)
sashi-agemas', -ageru presents ; holds up
sashimas', sasu 1. points to ; holds umbrella 2. stabs, stings
sasoimas', sasou invites ; tempts
satō sugar
satsu[1] a volume, a book
satsu[2] paper money, a bill
satsujin murder
sawagimas', sawagu makes lots of noise, clamors
sawarimas', sawaru touches
sayonara goodby
sebiro business suit
sei[1] height, stature

sei[2] 1. nature 2. sex

sei[3] cause ; due to...

-sei made in ...

seibu the west, the western part

seifu government

seifuku uniform

seiji politics

seikatsu life

seikō success

seinen young man, youth

seiryoku power, energy ; influence

seisan production, manufacture

seiseki results, marks

seishiki formal, formality

seishin soul, mind, spirit

seishitsu character, disposition

seito pupil, student

seitō political party

seiyō the West, the Occident, Europe and America

seizei at most, at best

seizō production, manufacture

seizon existence

sekai world

seken the public, people, the world

seki[1] cough

seki[2] seat

Sekijūji Red Cross

sekinin responsibility, obligation

sekitan coal

sekiyu kerosene, petroleum
sekkaku especially ; with much trouble
sekken soap
semai narrow
sembei rice-crackers
semete at least ; at most
semmenki wash basin
semmon specialty, major (line)
sempō the other side
sempūki electric fan
sen[1] thousand
sen[2] line, route
sen[3] plug, cork, stopper
sen[4] (**-to**) cents
senden propaganda, publicity
sengetsu last month
sengo postwar
sen-in member of the crew ; ship's crew
senji wartime
senkyo election
senryō military occupation
sensei teacher ; Dr. ...
senshu athlete ; champion
senshū last week
sensō war, battle
sentaku[1] washing, laundry
sentaku[2] selection, choice
senzen prewar
seppuku harakiri

seri auction
serifu one's lines (in a play), dialogue
sētā sweater
setomono pottery, chinaware
Seto-naikai The Inland Sea
setsubi equipment, facilities
setsumei explanation
setsuna moment, instant
sewa 1. care, trouble, assistance 2. meddling, minding other people's business
sewashii busy
-sha company
shaberimas', shaberu chatters
shabon soap
shaburimas', shaburu sucks, chews
shachō president of a company, boss
shadan corporation
shadō road, roadway, driveway
shagamimas', shagamu squats, crouches on heels
sha-in employee
shakai society, social
shakkuri hiccup
shako garage, car-barn
shan pretty, handsome
share joke, pun
shashin photo, picture
shashō conductor
shatsu undershirt
shawā shower

shi[1] death
shi[2]**=yon** four
shi[3] city
shi[4] poetry
... shi Mr. ...
... shi, and
shiagemas', shiageru finishes up
shiai match, contest, meet
shiasatte three days from now
shiawase luck, fortune
shiba 1. turf, lawn 2. brushwood
shibai play (drama)
shibaraku for a while
Shibaraku des' ne. It's nice to see you again.
shibarimas', shibaru ties up
shibashiba often, repeatedly
shibiremas', shibireru goes numb, (a leg, etc.) falls asleep
shibori, o-shibori a wet towel (wrung out)
shiborimas', shiboru wrings out, squeezes
shibui 1. puckery, astringent 2. wry; glum 3. severely simple, tastefully bare
shichi[1] seven
shichi[2] something pawned
shichi-jū seventy
shichimen-chō turkey
shichiya pawnbroker, pawnshop
shichō mayor
shichū stew

shidai circumstances; as soon as
shidan army division
shidashiya caterer
shigai outskirts of city, suburbs
shigaretto cigarette
shigatsu April
shigeki stimulation
shigoto job, work, undertaking
shigure drizzle
shihai management, control
shiharai paying out
shihon capital, funds
shiji support, maintenance
shijin poet
shi-jū forty
shijū all the time
shika deer
...shika except for, only, but
shikaku, sh'kaku 1. square 2. qualification, competency
shikarimas', shikaru scolds
shikashi, **sh'kashi** but, however
shikata (sh'kata) ga arimasen there's nothing we can do about it
shiken, sh'ken examination, test
shikimono spread; a rug, a cushion
shikkari firmly, resolutely
shikki dampness
shikko urinate (child's word)

shikimas', shiku spreads; sits on
shima[1] island
shima[2] stripes
shimaimas', shimau puts away, finishes
shimas', suru does
shimasen doesn't
shimash'ta did
Shimatta! Damn!
shimbun newspaper
shimemas', shimeru closes
shimerimas', shimeru is damp
shimeshimas', shimesu shows. indicates
shimi stain, blot
shimimas', shimiru penetrates, smarts
shimin citizen
shimo frost
shimpai worry, uneasiness
shimpo progress
shin 1. core, pith, heart 2. heart, spirit
shina articles, goods; quality
Shina China
shindai bed, berth
shingō signal
shinimas', shinu dies
shinja a believer; a Christian
shinjimas', shinjiru believes in, trusts
shinju pearl
shinkei nerve
shinnen new year

shinobimas', shinobu bears, puts up with
shinrai trust, confidence
shinri 1. psychology 2. truth
shinrui relative
shinsatsu medical examination
shinsetsu kind, cordial
shinu (shinimas') dies
shin-yō trust, confidence; credit
shinzō heart
shio 1. salt 2. tide
shippai failure, blunder, defeat
shippo tail
shirabemas', shiraberu investigates, examines
shirami louse
shirase report, notice
shireikan commandant, headquarters
shiri buttocks, bottom, seat
shirimas', shiru knows
shiro (o-shiro) castle
shiroi white
shirōto amateur
shiru[1] juice, gravy; broth, soup
shiru[2] **(shirimas')** knows
shirushi indication, sign, symptom; effect
shiryo consideration, thought(-fulness)
shishi lion
shisō thought, concept
shita, sh'ta[1] bottom, below, under
shita, sh'ta[2] tongue

shita, sh'ta[3] did, has done

shitagatte according to, in conformity with

shitaku, sh'taku preparation, arrangement

shitashii intimate, familiar

shitate-ya tailor

shite, sh'te doing; does and

shiten branch shop

shitsu quality, nature

shitsubō disappointment

shitsugyō unemployment

shitsumon question

shitsurei discourtesy, impoliteness

shitsuren disappointment in love

shitte imas' knows

shiwa wrinkle, crease, fold

shiwaza act, deed

shiyō 1. use, employment 2. method, means, way

shizen nature, natural

shizuka quiet, still

shizumimas', shizumu sinks

shō nature, disposition, quality

shōbai trade, business

shōben urine, urinate

shōbō fire-fighting

shōbu match, game, contest

shobun, shochi management, disposition, dealing with

shōchi agreement

Shōchi shimash'ta. Yes, sir.

shōchō symbol

shōga ginger
shōgai impediment, obstacle, hindrance
shōgakkō primary (elementary) school
shōgakusei primary school children
shōgi chess
shōgyō commerce, trade
shōhi consumption, spending
shōhin goods, merchandise
shoimas', shou carries on back, shoulders
shōjiki honest
shoki secretary
shōki sober; in one's right mind
shōkin 1. hard cash 2. prize money; reward 3. indemnity, reparation
shokki table service (ware)
shokki-dana pantry, dish-cupboard
shokkō factory-worker; workman
shōko proof, evidence
shōkō commissioned officer
shoku 1. office, occupation 2. food
shokubutsu (botanical) plant
shokudō dining room; restaurant
shokudō-sha dining car, diner
shokuen table salt
shokugyō occupation, profession
shokuhin groceries
shokuji meal
shokumotsu food
shokuryō-hin groceries

shokuyoku appetite
shomei signature
shōnen boy, lad, youngster
shōni infant, child
shōnin merchant, trader
shōrai future
shōrei encouragement, stimulation, promotion
shori managing, disposing of, transacting, dealing with
shōryaku abbreviation
shōsa major; lieutenant commander
shosai study, library (room)
shoseki books, publications
shōsetsu fiction, novel
shōshō = **chotto**
shōsoku news, word from
shotai housekeeping; a household
shōtai invitation
shotchū all the time
shoten bookshop
shōten focus
shotō islands
shotoku income, gain
shotoku-zei income tax
shōtotsu collision
shou (**shoimas'**) carries on back, shoulders
shōyo bonus, prize, reward
shoyū possession, one's own
shōyu soy sauce
shozai whereabouts

shū(-kan) week
shuchō shimas' asserts, claims, maintains
shudan ways, means, measures, steps
shūdan group, collective body
shufu 1. housewife 2. capital city
shugeki attack, charge
shugi principle, doctrine, -ism
shūi circumference; surroundings
shujin boss, master; husband
shuju all kinds of
shujutsu operation, surgery
shūkan custom, practice, habit
shukudai homework
shukuga congratulation
shū-kuriimu a cream puff, an eclair
shūmai small Chinese meat-filled pastries
shūmatsu weekend
shumi taste, interest
shunkan a moment, an instant
shuppan publishing
shuppatsu departure
shūri repair
shurui kind, sort
shūsen(-go) (after) the end of the war
shūshin ethics, morals
shūshoku getting a job
shusse making a success out of life
shusseki attendance, presence
shutchō a business trip, an official tour

shūten terminus
shuyō leading, chief
shūzen repair
sō 1. that's right, yes 2. that way, like that
Sō des' ka. 1. Oh? How interesting! 2. Is that right?
soba[1] side, near
soba[2] (**o-soba**) buckwheat noodles
sōbetsu farewell; send-off
soboku simple, naive, unsophisticated
sōchi equipment, apparatus
sochira 1. there, that way 2. that one
sōdan consultation, conference, advice, talk
sodatemas', sodateru raises, rears, educates
sodachimas', sodatsu grows up, is raised (reared)
sode sleeve
soemas', soeru adds, throws in extra, attaches
sofu grandfather
sofuto(-kuriimu) "soft ice cream" = frozen custard
sōgo mutual, reciprocal
sōi discrepancy, difference
soimas', sou runs along, follows
soitsu that one
sōji cleaning, sweeping
sōji-fu cleaning lady (man)
sōji-ki a sweeper
sōjū shimas' manipulates, handles, controls, operates
sōkei the grand total
sokki shorthand

sokkuri entirely, completely; just like
soko[1] there, that place
soko[2] bottom
sokudo, sokuryoku speed
sokutatsu special delivery
somatsu crude, coarse
somemas', someru dyes
son damage, loss, disadvantage
sonaemas', sonaeru prepares, fixes, installs, furnishes; possesses
songai damage, harm
sonkei respect, esteem
sonna such (a), that kind of
sonnara then, in that case
sono that
son-shimas', -suru 1. incurs loss 2. exists
sonzai existence
soppa buckteeth
sora sky
sora de by heart, from memory
sorashimas', sorasu 1. dodges, turns aside 2. warps
sore that one, it
soremas', soreru deviates, strays, digresses
Soren Soviet Russia
sori 1. warp, curve, bend 2. sled
sōri-daijin prime minister, premier
sorimas', soru 1. shaves 2. bends, warps
sōritsu establishment
soroban abacus, counting beads

soroemas', soroeru puts in order; collects; completes a set
soroi a set of something
soroimas', sorou are arranged in order; gather together; make a set
sōron quarrel, dispute
sorosoro little by little
soru (sorimas') 1. shaves 2. bends, warps
soshiki system, structure
sōshiki funeral
soshō lawsuit
sōshoku ornament, decoration
sosogimas', sosogu pours (into)
sōsu sauce; gravy
sotchi = sochira
soto outside, outdoors
sōtō 1. rather, quite, fairly 2. suitable, proper
... (ni) sotte along the ...
sou (soimas') runs along, follows
sōzō imagination
su 1. nest 2. vinegar
sū number; numeral
suashi barefoot
subarashii wonderful
subekkoi slippery, slick, smooth
suberimas' suberu, slides, slips, skates
subete all
sue 1. end, close 2. future
sufu staple fiber
sūgaku mathematics

sugata form, figure, shape
sugi cryptomeria, Japanese cedar
. . . -sugi past (the hour)
sugimas', sugiru passes; exceeds; overdoes
sugoi 1. swell, wonderful, terrific 2. dreadful, ghastly, weird
sugoku terribly
sugu ni at once, immediately
suguremas', sugureru is excellent; surpasses
suidō waterworks, water service
suiei swimming
suifu seaman, sailor
suigara cigarette (cigar) butt
suihei[1] navy man, sailor, seaman
suihei[2] horizon; water level
suimas', suu sips, sucks, smokes, breathes in
suimin(-zai) sleep(ing pills)
suiyōbi Wednesday
suji tendon; muscle; fiber; line; plot
sūji numeral, figure
sukebe, s'kebe oversexed, wolfish
suki, s'ki[1] is liked
suki, s'ki[2]**(-ma)** crack; opening; opportunity
suki, s'ki[3] a plow
sukimas', suku 1. likes 2. plows 3. combs
sukkari completely, all
sukoshi, s'koshi a little, a bit
sukunai few, meager
sukuimas', sukuu helps, rescues, saves
sumai residence

sumashimas', sumasu 1. finishes, concludes 2. puts up with (things as they are)
sumi[1] an inside corner
sumi[2] 1. charcoal 2. India ink
sumō Japanese wrestling
sumimas', sumu 1. comes to an end 2. lives
Sumimasen. 1. Excuse me. 2. Thank you.
sumpō measurements
suna sand
sunawachi namely, to wit; that is to say; in other words
sune shin, leg
supōtsu, s'pōts' sports, athletics
suppai sour
suremas', sureru it rubs, grazes
suri pickpocket
surimas', suru 1. rubs; files; grinds 2. prints 3. picks one's pockets
suru (shimas') does
sushi (o-sushi) pickled-rice tidb
suso skirt (of mountain); hem
susu soot
susumemas', susumeru encourages, recommends, advises, persuades, urges
susumimas', susumu goes forward, progresses; goes too fast, gets ahead
sutando, s'tando a stand; gas station; desk lamp, floor lamp
suteki, s'teki fine, splendid, swell
sutekki, s'tekki walking stick, cane

sutemas', suteru throws away, abandons
sutēshon, s'tēshon railroad station
suto, s'to (sutoraiki) strike
sutōbu, s'tōbu stove, heater
suu (suimas') sips, sucks, smokes, breathes in
suwarimas', suwaru sits (especially Japanese style)
suzu 1. tin 2. little bells
suzume sparrow
suzushii cool

T

ta rice-field
taba bundle, bunch
tabako cigarettes; tobacco
tabemas', taberu eats
tabemono food
tabi[1] Japanese split-toe socks
tabi[2] journey, trip
. . . tabi ni every time...
tabi-tabi often
tabun 1. probably, likely; perhaps 2. a lot
tachi nature, disposition
tachiba viewpoint, standpoint, situation
tachi-domarimas', -domaru stops, stands still
Tachiiri Kinshi No Trespassing
tachimas', tatsu 1 stands up; leaves 2. elapses 3. cuts off
tada 1. only, just 2. (for) free 3. ordinary

tadaima just now; in a minute
Tadaima (kaerimashita)! I'm back! (said on returning to one's residence)
tadashii proper, correct, honest
taema-naku, taezu continuously, without interruption
taemas', taeru 1. bears, puts up with; 2. ceases
taga a barrel hoop
tagai (ni) mutual(ly)
-tagarimas', -tagaru wants to, is eager to
tai- 1. versus, towards, against 2. big, great
tai[1] sea bream, red snapper
tai[2] form, style; body
tai[3] belt; zone
-tai wants to, is eager to
taifū typhoon
taigai 1. in general; for the most part; practically 2. probably, like, like as not
Taiheiyō Pacific Ocean
taihen 1. very, exceedingly, terribly 2. serious; disastrous; enormous
taii army captain; navy lieutenant
taiiku physical education, athletics
taikai 1. ocean, high sea 2. mass meeting; convention
taikaku body build, physique
taikei a system
taiken personal experience
taiko drum
taikutsu boring, dull
taiman negligent, careless, neglectful

taimen 1. sense of honor, "face" 2. interview
taira even, smooth, flat
tairiku continent
taisa 1. army colonel; navy captain 2. a great difference
Taiseiyō Atlantic Ocean
taisen a great war, a world war
taisetsu important; precious
taishi ambassador
taishi-kan embassy
tai-shita (**-sh'ta**) important; serious; immense
. . . ni tai-sh'te against; toward
taishō 1. general; admiral 2. contrast
taishū the general public, the masses; popular
taisō calisthenics, physical exercises
Taiwan Formosa
taiya a tire
taiyō 1. ocean 2. sun 3. summary
taka 1. hawk 2. quantity
takai high; loud
takara a treasure
take bamboo
take-no-ko bamboo shoot
taki waterfall
taki-bi bonfire
taki-gi firewood, fuel
taki-tsuke kindling
takimas', taku makes a fire; cooks; burns
tako 1. octopus 2. kite 3. callus, corn
taku (**takimas'**) makes a fire; cooks; burns

taku 1. house ; husband 2. table, desk
takumi skill
tak'san, takusan lots
takuwaemas', takuwaeru saves up, hoards
tama 1. ball ; globe ; bulb ; bullet 2. jewel; bead ; drop 3. round thing ; coin ; slug
tama ni rarely, occasionally, seldom
tamago egg
tamaranai, tamarimasen can't stand it; is intolerable
tamarimas', tamaru it accumulates
tamashii soul, spirit
tamatama occasionally
tamatsuki billiards
tambo rice-field
tame 1. for the sake (good, benefit) of 2. for the purpose of 3. because (of)
tamemas', tameru accumulates it
tameshimas', tamesu tries, attempts, experiments with
tammono draperies, dry goods
tamoto sleeve ; edge, end
tamochimas', tamotsu keeps, preserves
tampopo dandelion
tamushi ringworm ; athlete's foot
tana shelf, rack
tane 1. seed 2. source, cause 3. material 4. secret, trick to it 5. subject, topic
tango words, vocabulary
tan-i unit
tani(-ma) valley

tanjōbi birthday
tanomimas', tanomu 1. begs, requests 2. relies upon; entrusts with 3. hires, engages (a professional man)
tanoshii pleasant, enjoyable
tanoshimimas', tanoshimu enjoys
tansan(-sui) soda water
tansu chest of drawers
tantei detective
tanuki 1. badger 2. sly person
tanzen=dotera padded bathrobe
taoremas', taoreru falls down, tumbles, collapses
taoru towel
taoshimas', taosu knocks down, overthrows
tappuri fully, more than enough
tara cod (fish)
...-tara if
tarai tub, basin
tarappu gangway
tarashimas', tarasu 1. seduces; wheedles 2. hangs, dangles; drops, spills
taremas', tareru hangs down, dangles; drips
tarimas, tariru is enough, suffices
taru barrel, keg
tarumimas', tarumu gets slack (loose), relaxed
taryō large quantity
tashika, tash'ka for sure; safe
tashikamemas', tashikameru makes sure, ascertains
tassha healthy; skillful, good at

tasshimas', tassuru accomplishes; reaches;
tasū large number ; majority ⌈lieved
tasukarimas', tasukaru is saved ; is re-
tasukemas', tasukeru 1. helps 2. saves
tasuki a sleeve cord
tatakaimas', tatakau fights
tatakimas', tataku strikes, hits
tatami floor-matting
tatamimas', tatamu folds up
tate ni lengthwise, vertically
-tate (no) fresh from...
tate-fuda signboard
tate-mashi house extension, annex
tatemas', tateru erects, builds ; sets up,
tatemono building ⌊establishes
tatoeba for example, for instance ⌈off
tatsu 1. stands up ; leaves 2. elapses 3. cuts
taue rice-planting
tawara straw bag ; bale
tawashi scrubbing-brush ; swab
tayori communication, correspondence, a letter, word from
tayorimas', tayoru relies on, depends on
tazunemas', tazuneru 1. asks (a question) 2. visits 3. looks for
te hand, arm ; trick, move ; kind ⌈ing
. . . -te GERUND : does and, is and ; doing, be-
teate treatment ; reparation, provision ; al-
tebukuro gloves ⌊lowance

tēburu table ; **-kake** table-cloth
tegakari a hold, a place to hold on ; a clue, the track of
tegami letter
tegata a note, a bill
te-gatai safe ; reliable ; steady
tegokoro discretion
teguchi way (of doing things), trick
tehazu arrangements
tehon model, pattern
tei- fixed, appointed
teian proposal, suggestion
teibō dike, embankment
teiden failure (stoppage) of electricity
teido degree, extent
teika the set price
teiki (no) fixed, regular, periodical
teikoku empire, imperial
teinei polite ; careful
te-ire repair ; upkeep
teisai appearance, get-up, form
teisha stopping (of a vehicle)
teishi suspension, interruption
teishoku the regular meal ; table d'hote
teishu host ; landlord ; husband
tejun order, procedure, program
tekazu trouble
teki enemy, opponent, rival
-teki a drop
tekido moderation

tekigi suitable, fit
tekisetsu appropriate, to the point
tekishimas'. tekisuru is suitable, qualified
tekis'to. tekisuto text (book)
tekitō suitable
tekki(-ten) hardware (store)
tekkyō iron bridge
teko lever
te-kubi wrist
tema time ; trouble
temae this side ; me, I
temane gesture
temaneki beckoning
temawari personal effects ; luggage
. . . -te mo even if...
tempi oven
tempura anything fried in batter, especially shrimp
ten 1. point, dot 2. sky, heaven
-ten shop
tengu 1. a long-nosed goblin 2. conceited person
te-nimotsu hand luggage
ten-in shop clerk
tenjō ceiling
tenki 1. weather 2. nice weather
tennen natural
Tennō (sama) the Emperor
tensai genius
tensei disposition, temperament
tenshi angel

te-nugui hand towel
te-ono hatchet
teppen top
teppō rifle
tēpu tape
tera Buddhist temple
terebi television
teremas', tereru feels embarrassed, awkward, flustered
terimas', teru it shines
tesage handbag
tesū trouble
tetsu iron, steel
tetsudaimas', tetsudau helps
tetsudō railroad
tetsugaku philosophy
tetsuzuki formalities, procedure
tettei-teki thorough
to door
tō 1. ten 2. rattan, cane 3. tower, pagoda
tō- 1. the current, the appropriate 2. east
Tō-a East Asia
tobashimas', tobasu lets fly; skips, omits; hurries
tobimas', tobu jumps; flies
tobira a door of a gate
toboshii scarce, meager, scanty
tobu (tobimas') jumps; flies
tōbun for the time being
tōchaku arrival
tochi ground; a piece of land

tochū on the way

tōdai 1. lighthouse 2. (T) Tokyo University

toden Tokyo streetcar service

todokemas', todokeru 1. delivers 2. notifies, reports

todokimas', todoku reaches ; arrives

todomarimas', todomaru it stops; it remains

todomemas', todomeru stops it

todorokimas', todoroku roars, rumbles

toei metropolitan (run by the metropolis of Tokyo)

tōfu bean curd

togamemas', togameru blames, reproves, finds fault with

togarashimas', togarasu sharpens, points

togarimas', togaru gets sharp (pointed)

toge thorn

tōge mountain pass

togemas', togeru achieves, accomplishes

togimas', togu grinds, sharpens, polishes

tōhyō ballot, vote

tōi far-off, distant

toimas', tou inquires

toire(tto) toilet

tōka 10 days ; 10th day

tokai city, town

tokashimas', tokasu melts (dissolves) it

tokei clock ; watch

tōkei statistics

tokemas', tokeru it melts (dissolves); comes undone ; gets solved

toki time

tōki 1. pottery, ceramics 2. registration
tokimas', toku 1. undoes, unties; solves
2. explains, persuades, preaches 3. combs
tokkuri saké bottle
tokkyū special express (train)
toko bed
tokonoma alcove in Japanese room ⌈time
tokoro 1. place 2. address 3. circumstance,
toku[1] 1. virtue 2. profit, advantage, gain
toku[2] **(tokimas')** 1. undoes, unties; solves
2. explains, persuades, preaches 3. combs
toku[3] special
tokubetsu special, particular, extra
tokui 1. pride 2. specialty 3. customer
toku-nitō special 2nd class
tokushoku special feature, characteristic
tokushu (tokuyū) special, particular
tōkyoku the authorities ⌈overnight
tomarimas', tomaru 1. it stops 2. stays
tombo dragonfly ⌈person up overnight
tomemas', tomeru 1. stops it 2. puts a
tomimas', tomu is rich in
tomma idiot, fool
tomo together; company; friend
. . . to mo! Of course...
tomonaimas', tomonau accompanies
tōmorokoshi corn
tomoshimas', tomosu burns (a light)
tomu (tomimas') is rich in

tonaemas', tonaeru advocates ; shouts ; recites ; calls ; claims
tōnan southeast
tonari next-door, neighbor(ing) ⌈shocking
tonde-mo-nai, (tonda) outrageous, terrible,
ton-katsu breaded pork cutlet
to-ni-kaku nevertheless
toppatsu outbreak
tora tiger
toraemas', toraeru catches, seizes
torakku 1. truck 2. track
torampu playing cards
tori 1. chicken 2. bird
tori- VERB PREFIX : takes and...
... tōri just as ... ⌈thing)
tōri avenue ; passage ; way (of doing some-
tori-atsukaimas', -atsukau handles, deals
tori-awase assortment ⌊with
tori-hiki transaction, deal, business
torii gate to a Shinto shrine
tori-keshimas', -kesu cancels, revokes
torimas', toru takes ; takes away
tōrimas', tōru passes by, passes through ; penetrates ⌈3. agency 4. transmit
toritsugi 1. answering the door 2. an usher
tōrō a stone lantern
tōroku registration
tōron debate, discussion
toru (**torimas'**) takes ; takes sway

tōru (**tōrimas'**) passes by, passes through; penetrates
Toruko (**-buro**) Turkey; Turkish (bath)
toshi[1] 1. age 2. year
toshi[2] city
tōshimas', tōsu lets through (in), admits; shows in; pierces, penetrates
toshi-shita younger
... to sh'te (**shite**) as, by way of
toshi-ue older
toshiyori an old person
tosho-kan library (building)
tosho-shitsu library (room)
toso spiced saké drunk at New Year's (mulled wine)
tōsu (**tōshimas'**) lets through (in), admits; shows in; pierces, penetrates
to(t)temo terribly, extremely, completely
totonoemas', totonoeru regulates, adjusts; prepares
totonoimas', totonou is in order; is ready
totsuzen suddenly
totte handle
... ni totte for, to
totte kimas' (**kuru**) brings
totte ikimas' (**iku**) takes
tou (**toimas'**) inquires
tōwaku embarrassment, dilemma
Tōyō the East, the Orient
to yū which says; which is (called), called

tozan mountain climbing
tōzen naturally ; proper, deserved
tsū authority, expert
tsuba spit, saliva
tsubaki camellia
tsubame swallow (bird)
tsubasa wing
tsubo 1. jar 2. 6 sq. ft. ⌈is shut
tsubomarimas', tsubomaru is puckered up ;
tsubomemas', tsubomeru puckers it up ;
tsubomi flower bud ⌊shuts
tsubu grain ; drop ⌈es)
tsuburemas', tsubureru it collapses (smash-
tsubushimas', tsubusu smashes (crushes) it
tsuchi 1. earth, ground 2. hammer
tsūchi report, notice
tsue cane, walking stick
tsuge boxwood
tsugemas', tsugeru tells, informs
tsugi 1. next ; following 2. patch
tsugimas', tsugu 1. pours 2. patches 3. inherits, succeeds to 4. joins, grafts, glues
tsugi-me joint, seam
tsugi-tsugi one after another ⌈nity
tsugō circumstances, convenience, opportu-
tsui[1] 1. just now 2. unintentionally
tsui[2] a pair
tsuide 1. opportunity, convenience 2. order
tsuihō purge

tsui-ni at last; after all
...ni tsuite about, concerning
tsūji 1. bowel activity 2. effect
tsūjimas', tsūjiru gets through; communicates; transmits; connects, runs; is understood; is well versed in
...o tsūjite through the good offices of...
tsūjō usual, ordinary
tsuka 1. mound 2. hilt
tsukaemas'[1]**, tsukaeru** serves; is useful
tsukaemas',[2] **tsukaeru** is obstructed, clogged up, busy
tsukai, ts'kai 1. message, errand 2. messenger, errand boy ┌handles
tsukaimas', tsukau uses; spends; employs,
tsukamimas', tsukamu seizes, grasps
tsukaremas', tsukareru gets tired
tsukemono pickles
tsukemas', tsukeru 1. attaches, sticks on, adds; turns on (lights); puts on, wears; applies 2. pickles; soaks
tsuki, ts'ki moon ┌ship
tsukiai association, social company, friend-
tsuki-aimas', -au associates with, enjoys the company of
tsuki-atarimas', -ataru runs into; comes to the end of ┌sticks it out
tsuki-dashimas', -dasu makes protrude,
tsuki-demas', -deru protrudes, sticks out

tsukimas',[1] **tsukiru** comes to an end, runs out

tsukimas',[2] **tsuku** comes in contact; sticks to ; joins ; follows ; touches ; arrives ; burns, is on

tsukimas',[3] **tsuku** stabs, thrusts, pushes

tsukurimas', tsukuru makes; builds; writes

tsukuroimas', tsukurou repairs, mends

tsukushimas', tsukusn exhausts, runs out of ; exerts oneself, strives

tsuma wife

tsumamimas', tsumamu pinches, picks ; summarizes

tsumamimono things to nibble on (with one's fingers) while drinking

tsumaranai worthless, no good

tsumari after all ; in short

tsumarimas', tsumaru is clogged up, choked; is stuck; is shortened; is crammed

tsumbo deaf

tsume claw, nail, hoof

tsumemas', tsumeru stuffs, crams ; cans

tsumetai cold (to the touch)

tsumi crime, sin, guilt, fault

tsumimas', tsumu 1. piles it up, accumulates it ; deposits ; loads 2. gathers, plucks, clips

tsumori expectation, intention

tsuna rope. cord, cable

tsunagimas', tsunagu connects, links, ties

tsune usual, ordinary

tsuno horn (of an animal)
tsura face
tsurai painful, cruel
tsure company, companion
tsuremas', tsureru brings along, is accompanied by
tsuri 1. (small) change 2. fishing
tsuriai balance, equilibrium, symmetry
tsurigane temple bell
tsurimas', tsuru[1] 1. hangs 2. fishes
tsūro passage, thoroughfare
tsuru[2] 1. vine 2. earpieces of glasses frame 3. string (of bow or violin) 4. handle
tsūshin correspondence ; news
tsutaemas', tsutaeru passes it on to someone else ; reports, communicates ; transmits ; hands down
tsutawarimas', tsutawaru is passed on (reported, communicated, transmitted, handed down)
tsutomemas', tsutomeru 1. is employed, works 2. exerts oneself, strives
tsutsu cylinder, pipe ; gun
tsutsumi 1. package, bundle 2. dike, embankment
tsutsumimas', tsutsumu wraps it up
tsutsushimi prudence, discretion
tsuttsukimas', tsuttsuku pecks at
tsuya gloss, shine
tsūyaku interpreter ; interpreting

tsuyoi strong; brave

tsuyu 1. dew 2. rainy season 3. light soup

tsuzukemas', tsuzukeru continues it

tsuzukimas', tsuzuku it continues

tsuzumemas', tsuzumeru reduces, cuts down, summarizes

tsuzurimas', tsuzuru 1. spells 2. composes, writes 3. patches; binds; sews (together)

U

u cormorant (fishing bird)

ubaimas', ubau seizes, robs, plunders

uchi 1. house, home; family 2. inside; among

uchi- VERB PREFIX: hits and, takes and

uchiki shy, timid

uchimas', utsu strikes, hits; sends a telegram; fires, shoots

uchiwa a flat fan

ude arm

ude-kubi wrist

ude-wa bracelet

udon Japanese noodles

ue above, upper; on, on top of

ueki-ya gardener

uemas', ueru 1. plants, grows 2. starves

ugokashimas', ugokasu moves it

ugokimas', ugoku it moves

uguisu nightingale

uji family, clan ; family name
ukabimas', ukabu floats
ukagaimas', ukagau 1. visits 2. asks a question 3. hears 4. looks for
ukai 1. cormorant fishing 2. detour
ukemas', ukeru receives; accepts; takes; gets ; suffers
uke-tori receipt
uke-tsuke information desk ; receptionist
ukimas', uku floats
ukkari absentmindedly
uma horse
umai 1. tasty, delicious 2. skillful, good 3. successful ; profitable
umaremas', umareru is born
ume plum tree
ume-boshi pickled plum
umemas', umeru buries ; fills up ; plugs
umi 1. sea 2. pus
umimas', umu 1. gives birth to 2. festers
ummei destiny
umpan transportation
un fate, luck
unagashimas', unagasu stimulates, urges (on)
unagi eel
unazukimas', unazuku nods
undō 1. movement 2. exercise ; sports ; athletics
undō-ba, (-jō) gymnasium ; athletic field
unga canal
unsō transportation

unten operation, running, working, driving
unten-shu driver, operator
uo fish
ura[1] back (side); lining; what's behind it; the alley
ura[2] bay
ura-girimas', -giru betrays
ura-guchi back door
urami grudge, resentment, ill will
uranai fortunetelling; fortuneteller
uremas', ureru it sells, is in demand; thrives; is popular
ureshii delightful, pleasant, wonderful
uri melon
uri-dashi (special) sale
uri-kake credit sales
uriko shopgirl; salesman; peddler; newsboy
urimas', uru sells
urimono something for sale
uru wool
urusai annoying
urushi lacquer
usagi rabbit
ushi cow, cattle
ushiro behind; (in) back
uso lie, fib
usu mortar
usui thin, pale, weak
uta song; poem
utagaimas', utagau doubts

utaimas', utau sings ; recites
utsu (**uchimas'**) strikes, hits ; sends a telegram ; fires, shoots
utsukushii beautiful
utsurimas'. utsuru 1. it moves, shifts, changes 2. is reflected, can be seen (through); is becoming
utsushimas', utsusu 1. moves (transfers) it; infects, gives another person a disease 2. copies; takes a picture of; projects a picture
utsuwa 1. receptacle 2. tool 3. ability
uttaemas', uttaeru accuses, sues
uttōshii gloomy, dismal
uwabaki slippers
uwabe surface ; outer appearances
uwa-gaki address
uwagi coat, jacket
uwagoto raving, delirium
uwaki fickle
uwasa rumor, gossip
uyamaimas', uyamau reveres, respects

W

wa circle ; wheel ; link ; ring ; loop
... wa as for (DE-EMPHASIZES PRECEDING WORD)
wa- Japanese
wabi apology

wabishii miserable ; lonely
wadai topic of conversation
wa-fuku, wa-f'ku Japanese clothes
waga-mama selfish
wairo bribery ; graft
waisetsu obscenity
waishatsu shirt
wakai young
wakaremas', wakareru they part, separate ; it branches off, splits
wakarimas', wakaru it is clear (understood) ; understands ; has good sense
wakashimas', wakasu boils it
wake 1. reason 2. meaning 3. case, circumstance
wakemas', wakeru divides (splits, distributes) it ; separates them
waki side (of the chest)
wakimas', waku[1] 1. it boils 2. it gushes springs forth
waku[2] 1. frame ; crate 2. reel
wakuchin vaccine
wampaku naughty
wan 1. bowl 2. bay
wana trap, lasso
wani crocodile, alligator
wanisu varnish
wan-wan bow-wow !
wappu allotment, instalment
wara rice straw
waraimas', warau laughs

ware oneself ; me
waremas', wareru it cracks, it splits
ware-ware we ; us
wariai rate, percentage ; comparatively, relatively
waribiki discount
wari-kan going Dutch ; splitting the bill
wari-mae share, portion
warimas', waru divides it, breaks it, dilutes it
warui 1. bad 2. at fault
waru-kuchi(-guchi) abuse, scolding, slander
wasabi horseradish
washi 1. eagle 2. Japanese paper
wa-shoku Japanese food
wasuremono 1. leaving something behind 2. a thing left behind
wasuremas', wasureru forgets
wata 1. cotton 2. (=**hara-wata**) guts, intestines
wata-ire cotton-padded (garment)
watakushi, watashi I, me
watarimas', wataru crosses over
watashi-bune ferryboat
watashimas', watasu hands over, ferries
watashi-tachi we, us

Y

ya arrow
. . . ya and ; or
yā hi !, hello !

yabai dangerous (will get you into trouble)
yaban barbarian
yabo stupid ; rustic
yabu bush, thicket
yaburemas', yabureru it tears, bursts; is frustrated
yaburimas', yaburu tears (bursts) it ; frustrates ; violates ; defeats
yachin house rent
yado (-ya) inn
yaei camp, bivouac
yagai out in the country, out doors, in the field
yagate before long ; in time
yagi goat
yagu bedclothes ; over-quilt
yahari also ; either ; all the same
yaiba blade ; sword
yaji heckling
yakamashii noisy ; annoying ; over-strict
yakan teakettle
yake desperation
yakedo burn, scald (on the skin)
yakemas', yakeru it burns ; it is baked
yaki- roast
yakimas', yaku burns it ; bakes (roasts, toasts) it ; is jealous
yaki-mochi 1. jealousy 2. toasted rice-cake
yakimono pottery
yaki-pan toast
yakkai trouble, bother
yakkyoku pharmacy

yaku[1] (**yakimas'**) burns it; bakes (roasts, toasts) it; is jealous

yaku[2] approximately, about ⌈use, service

yaku[3] 1. office, post, duty 2. part, role 3.

yakuhin drugs; chemicals

yakume duty, function

yakunin government official

yakusho government office

yakuza no-good, worthless; coarse

yakuzai pharmaceuticals, medicines

yakyū baseball

yama 1. mountain 2. heap, pile 3. climax 4. speculation, venture

yamashii ashamed *or* guilty-feeling

yama-te, yamano-te uptown: the bluff area

Yamato Japan

yamemas', yameru stops it; abolishes; abstains from, gives up; resigns, quits

yami 1. darkness 2. disorder 3. black-marketing 4. anything illicit

yamimas', yamu it stops

yamome widow

yamu-o-enai unavoidable

yanagi willow

yane roof

yaoya greengrocer, vegetable market

yappashi also; either; all the same

... yara ... or something; what with ...

yari spear

yarimas', yaru 1. gives 2. sends 3. does
yarō scoundrel, so-and-so!
yasai vegetables
yasashii gentle; easy
yasemas', yaseru gets thin
yashi coconut
yashin ambition; treachery ┌nourishes
yashinaimas', yashinau brings up, rears;
yasui 1. cheap 2. easy 3. likely to, apt to
yasumi rest, break; vacation; holiday
yasumimas', yasumu rests, takes time off; stays away (from school); goes to bed,
yatoimas', yatou employs, hires └sleeps
yatsu guy, fellow, wretch; thing
yatto at last; barely, with difficulty
yattsu eight
yawarakai soft, mild
yaya a little; a little while
yayakoshii complicated; puzzling; tangled
yo 1. the world at large, the public 2. the age, the times; one's lifetime 3. night
yo- four
yō[1] manner, way; kind, sort
...no yō like, as if; seems like
yō[2] **(go-yō)** 1. business 2. use, service 3.
yō[3] gist └going to bathroom
yō- Western; American
yobi reserve ┌2. invites
yobimas', yobu 1. calls; names; summons

yobō precaution, prevention
yochi room, space, margin, leeway
yōdo iodine
yōfuku, yōf'ku (Western-style) clothes ; a suit ; a dress
yōfuku-ya tailor ; clothing shop
yogoremas', yogoreru gets soiled (dirty)
yogoshimas', yogosu soils, dirties, stains
yōgu tools, implements
yōhin imported goods
yohō forecast, prediction
yohodo considerably, a good deal
yoi[1] evening
yoi[2] = **ii** good
yōi preparation ; caution
yōiku bringing up, education
yoimas', you gets drunk ; gets seasick
yōji 1. business, errand 2. toothpick 3. infant
yōjin precaution, caution, care
yōka 8 days ; 8th day
yoke protection, shelter, screen
yokei superfluous, unnecessary, uncalled for
yokemas', yokeru avoids, keeps away from
yōki cheerful, bright, lively
yokin deposit (of money), bank account
yokka 4 days ; 4th day
yoko width ; sidewise
yokochō sidestreet, alley
yoko-girimas', -giru crosses, cuts across, intersects
yoku[1] greed

yoku[2] 1. well 2. lots, much 3. lots, often
yoku- the next (day, etc.)
yokubarimas', yokubaru is greedy
yōkyū demand, claim, request
yo-mawari night watchman
yome bride
yomimas', yomu reads
yōmō wool
yon four
yondokoro-nai inevitable
yo-nin 4 people
yopparaimas', yopparau gets drunk
yoppodo considerably, a good deal
...yori that ; from ; since ┌3. meet
yorimas', yoru 1. drops in 2. comes near
yorokobimas', yorokobu is happy, delighted
yoron public opinion
Yōroppa Europe
yoroshii very well ; excellent ┌best wishes
yoroshiku, yorosh'ku one's regards, one's
Dōzo yoroshiku. How do you do.
yoru[1] night ┌3. meet
yoru[2] **(yorimas')** 1. drops in 2. comes near
yosan budget, estimate
yōsan raising silkworms, silk farming
yosemas', yoseru 1. lets approach, brings near 2. collects, gathers 3. adds 4. sends
Yosh'! OK ! └5. makes (a crease)
yoshi reason ; meaning ; circumstance; means

yōshi forms, blanks, papers ⌈ing

yōshoku foreign (Western, American) cook-

yoshu foreign liquor

yoso somewhere else ; alien, strange

yosō expectation, presumption

yoshimas', **yosu** stops it

yōsu circumstances; aspect; appearance, look

yotamono hoodlum

yō-tashi business, errand

yotei expectation, plan

yōten gist, point

. . . ni yotte according to ; because of

yottsu four

you (**yoimas'**) gets drunk ; gets seasick

yowai weak ; frail ; easily intoxicated

yoyaku reservation, subscription, booking

yōyaku gradually ; at last ; barely

yoyū room, leeway, margin, excess, surplus

yu (**o-yu**) hot water, bath ; hot tea

yū (**iimas'**) says ; *see also* **to yū**

yūbe last night

yubi finger ; toe

yūbi elegant, graceful

yūbin mail

yūbin-kyoku post office

yubinuki thimble

yubiwa ring

yubi-zan finger counting

yubune bathtub

yūdachi a sudden shower
yudan negligence, carelessness, remissness
yudanemas', yudaneru entrusts, commits
Yudaya-jin Jew
Yudaya-kyō Judaism
yue reason, grounds
yūkan evening paper
yuki snow
...-yuki bound for
yukkuri slowly ; at ease
yūkō effective, valid
yuku=iku goes
yume dream
yūmei famous
yumi bow (for archery)
yumi-gata curve, arch, bow
yūmoa humor, wit
yunyū import(ing)
yūran excursion
yūrei ghost
yuremas', yureru it shakes, sways, rocks, rolls
yūretsu 1. quality 2. boldness
yuri lily
yūri profitable, advantageous
yurimas', yuru shakes it
yurui loose, slack ; lax, lenient ; slow
yurushimas', yurusu allows, permits, lets ; pardons, forgives
yūryoku strong, powerful, influential

yūshō victory, championship
yūshoku supper
yūshū melancholy
yushutsu export(ing)
yusō transport(ation)
yusuri blackmail, extortion
yutaka abundant, plentiful; wealthy
yutte saying; says and
yūutsu melancholy, gloom
yuwakashi teakettle
yūwaku temptation; seduction
yuzu orange
yuzurimas', yuzuru gives up; gives in; cedes; is inferior

Z

za 1. theater 2. seat
zabuton cushion to sit on
zadan chat
zai 1. lumber 2. material 3. talent 4. wealth
zai- (resident) in
zaibatsu the big financial groups
zaidan a foundation (philanthropical, etc.)
zaikai financial circles
zaimoku lumber, wood
zairu a mountain-climbing rope
zairyō raw material
zaisan property
zaisei finance

zakka miscellaneous goods, sundries

zambō slander

zange confession (of sins)

zankoku cruel, brutal

zannen regret, disappointed ; too bad

zara-ni found everywhere, very common

zara-zara rough

zaseki seat

zashiki room, living room

zasshi magazine, periodical

zassō weeds

zatsu- miscellaneous ; rough ; coarse

zatto roughly ; briefly

zehi 1. without fail, for sure 2. right or wrong

zei tax, customs

zeikan customs, custom house

zeikin tax

zeitaku luxury, extravagance

zembu all

zemmai 1. spring, hairspring 2. fern

zemmen 1. the entire surface 2. the front side

zemmetsu annihilation

zempō the front

zen- all, total, complete, the whole

zentai the whole body, the entirety

zento the future, prospects

zen-ya the night before

zenzen completely, utterly, entirely, altogether

zeppeki precipice

zerii jelly
zetsubō despair
zettai absolute(ly)
zō[1] statue, image, portrait
zō[2] elephant
zōdai enlargement, increase
zōgan inlaid work ; damascene
zōge ivory
zōho supplement
zōka increase, growth
zoku[1] common, vulgar ; popular
zoku[2] rebel ; thief
zokugo slang
zoku-shimas', -suru belongs
zokuzoku one right after another, in rapid succession
zombun as much as one likes
zongai beyond expectations
zōni rice-cakes boiled with vegetables (eaten at New Year's)
zonjimas', zonjiru thinks, feels ; knows
zonzai slovenly, rough, careless, sloppy
zōri straw sandals
zorozoro in a queue, all lined up
zōsen ship building
zōshin promotion, betterment, increase
zōsho book collection, library
zotto with a shiver (of horror)
zu picture, drawing, map, diagram
zuan sketch, design

zubon trousers, pants
zubon-shita underpants, shorts
zuhyō chart, diagram
zuibun 1. fairly, rather 2. quite, extremely
zuihitsu essays
zuii voluntary, optional
zukai illustration, diagram
-zuki a lover of ..., a great ... fan
zukku canvas ; duck
zukku-kutsu tennis shoes
zunō brains, head
zuremas', zureru slips out of place, gets loose
zurosu panties ; drawers
zuru cheating
zurui sly, cunning, tricky
... zutsu each, apiece
zutsū headache
zutto 1. directly 2. by far, much (more) 3. all through, all the time
zuzan sloppy, slipshod, careless
zūzūshii brazen, shameless, pushy

PART III

Writing Charts

NOTE: The following charts show the essentials of *kana* spelling. The squarish letters on the left are *katakana*, which is used to write foreign words and odd-sounding native words. The roundish letters on the right are the ones used for other words. In addition, modern Japanese use about 2000 characters of Chinese origin, called *kanji*. The first two charts show the simple syllables; the third shows those with the -y- element inserted. After these are notes on special combinations, such as long vowels and consonants. The Romanization in heavy black type is that used in this book. For some of the syllables, there are other ways of Romanizing them, and these are also shown, but in regular typeface.

ア あ **a**	カ か **ka**	サ さ **sa**	タ た **ta**	ナ な **na**	ハ は **ha**	マ ま **ma**	ヤ や **ya**	ラ ら **ra**	ワ わ **wa**	ン ん **-n -m.**
イ い **i**	キ き **ki**	シ し **shi** **sh'** si	チ ち **chi** **ch'** ti	ニ に **ni**	ヒ ひ **hi**	ミ み **mi**	—	リ り **ri**	ヰ ゐ (wi)	
ウ う **u**	ク く **ku** **k'**	ス す **su** **s'**	ツ つ **tsu** **ts'** tu	ヌ ぬ **nu**	フ ふ **fu** **f'** hu	ム む **mu**	ユ ゆ **yu**	ル る **ru**	—	
エ え **e**	ケ け **ke**	セ せ **se**	テ て **te**	ネ ね **ne**	ヘ へ **he**	メ め **me**	—	レ れ **re**	ヱ ゑ (we)	
オ お **o**	コ こ **ko**	ソ そ **so**	ト と **to**	ノ の **no**	ホ ほ **ho**	モ も **mo**	ヨ よ **yo**	ロ ろ **ro**	ヲ を (wo)	

バ ば ba	パ ぱ pa	ダ だ da	ザ ざ za	ガ が ga
ビ び bi	ピ ぴ pi	ヂ ぢ ji di	ジ じ ji zi	ギ ぎ gi
ブ ぶ bu	プ ぷ pu	ヅ づ zu du	ズ ず zu	グ ぐ gu
ベ べ be	ペ ぺ pe	デ で de	ゼ ぜ ze	ゲ げ ge
ボ ぼ bo	ポ ぽ po	ド ど do	ゾ ぞ zo	ゴ ご go

リャりゃ rya	ミャみゃ mya	ヒャひゃ hya	ニャにゃ nya	チャちゃ cha tya	シャしゃ sha sya	キャきゃ kya
リュりゅ ryu	ミュみゅ myu	ヒュひゅ hyu	ニュにゅ nyu	チュちゅ chu tyu	シュしゅ shu syu	キュきゅ kyu
リョりょ ryo	ミョみょ myo	ヒョひょ hyo	ニョにょ nyo	チョちょ cho tyo	ショしょ sho syo	キョきょ kyo
		ビャびゃ bya	ピャぴゃ pya	ヂャぢゃ ja dya	ジャじゃ ja zya	ギャぎゃ gya
		ビュびゅ byu	ピュぴゅ pyu	ヂュぢゅ ju dyu	ジュじゅ ju zyu	ギュぎゅ gyu
		ビョびょ byo	ピョぴょ pyo	ヂョぢょ jo dyo	ジョじょ jo zyo	ギョぎょ gyo

Long vowels are usually shown by repeating the vowel when writing in hiragana: **ā** ああ, **kā** かあ, **ū** うう, **fū** ふう, **ii** いい, **nii** にい, **ē** ええ, **tē** てえ.

In katakana, a single long stroke is often used (especially for foreign words): **ā** アー, **kā** カー, **ū** ウー, **fū** フー, **ii** イー, **nii** ニー, **e** エー, **tē** テー.

But in hiragana the long **ō** is usually written as if it were **ou** (for most, but not all, words): **ō** おう, **kō** こう, **sō** そう, **kyō** きょう, **yō** よう

Long consonants (**pp**, **tt**, **tch**, **kk**, **ss**, **ssh**) are written by inserting **tsu**, usually written smaller than the other letters: **kippu** きっぷ, **natte** なって, **botchan** ボッチャン, **gakkō** がっこう, **massugu** マッスグ, **issho** いっしよ.

But long **-mm-** and **-nn-** are written with ん and the appropriate symbol from the **ma** or **na** columns: **ammari** あんまり, **semmon** センモン, **annai** あんない, **san-nen** さんねん, **sam-myaku** さんみゃく.

PART IV

Money Conversion Tables